The Mayan Syndrome

The Mayan Syndrome

Gary Fincke

MadHat Press
Cheshire, Massachusetts

MadHat Press
MadHat Incorporated
PO Box 422, Cheshire, MA 01225

The Library of Congress has assigned
this edition a Control Number of
2023947182

ISBN 978-1-952335-67-9 (paperback)

Cover art and design by Marc Vincenz
Book design by MadHat Press

www.madhat-press.com

First Printing
Printed in the United States of America

This one is for everybody who has made a difference—
family, friends, teachers, and colleagues

Table of Contents

After the Three-Moon Era

The dozen fetuses of the sand shark feed on each other until only one is left to be born.

1

While eating breakfast, I read that some astronomers now believe Earth once had three moons. The scientists have a short list of hypotheses for two moons vanishing: They might have been sucked into the sun. They might have been shattered by the one moon that survived collision. Regardless, those other moons have vanished like glittering charms on a bracelet sliding off a child's wrist, the night sky empty with places where some arrangement of reflected light might have aligned itself against the darkness.

2

As a gift, decades ago, I had photographs of my father, his three brothers and sister restored, all of them originally taken when they were twenty-one. My father, beginning in his mid-eighties, pointed out how they had died in reverse order, beginning with his youngest brother. Each time I visited he made me examine that composite as if I had never seen it. "I'm the only one left," he said as he repeated their names, working backward toward himself. "Who would believe that?"

3

In early spring, when I visit during the year my father turns eighty-nine, he sings hymns aloud, tells me he wakes each morning expecting to be reborn, repeating it three times as if I'm the genie for resurrection. He says he hears the brothers I never had softly talking in the small bedroom where I slept while not one of them was born. They whisper, he says, about the way he refused them, saying "never" in the disciplined sign language of the rhythm method, keeping each of them a jealous spirit.

When he sings "In the Garden," I imagine those brothers, each day, rising to where my childhood window looks out at the rhododendron roof-high, the peace of its curtain, fragments of light that testify like character witnesses for weather. They move their mouths to those hymns that are heavy with sunrise and eternal joy.

The house holds the early darkness and the dry heat of the furnace, and my father repeats the chorus, raising his voice to be heard by those unborn boys who wake him each morning like birds.

4

One of my students tells me she devoured her twin in the womb, a doctor solving that natural crime with the spaced clues of ultrasound. "My mother explained it all to me," she says. "She gave me a copy of the ultrasound photograph that was taken when there were two of us."

She confides that she keeps her shadow twin sealed inside a scrapbook she opens on her birthday, leaving the photo face up in her bedroom. For when, she says, her family sings around her cake. For when their voices swell enough to reach her sister.

5

"The face seemed to warm up suddenly, sparkle returned to the eyes." So wrote a scientist named Robert Cornish in a report to the University of California in 1933. He was working on a way to revive the dead by strapping them to a seesaw and rapidly teeter-totting the corpses in order to circulate their blood.

A long time he and his assistants had spent at this primitive CPR, working the seesaw as if they were attempting to draw water from a long-unprimed pump. At least once, according to Cornish's report, their persistence brought a bit of color to the face of a recent heart-attack victim before it reverted to ashen.

Cornish needed to perfect his technique, but human bodies were hard to come by. He began to work with dogs, personally killing fox terriers, naming each of those freshly dead dogs Lazarus, referencing the optimism of the New Testament story. When some of those dogs breathed again, reviving for an hour or two before dying a second time, he was sure he was on to something.

Better yet, Lazarus IV and V lived for a few months. Newspapers reported the story. There was enough excitement and curiosity about his work that a movie was made that spliced in five minutes of footage of Cornish and his dogs. Lazarus IV and V, however, were blind and brain-damaged, inspiring, according to the newspaper stories, "terror in the ordinary dogs they met."[1]

6

On my next visit, as an early birthday present, I bring my father a gift, a book that traces the stories behind the composition of more than fifty selected hymns. The words and music for all of the hymns are included, and the book, with its dark, austere cover, has the feel of church about it, as if I should rise from my chair as he opens it, ready to join in singing the processional.

It's been eighteen years since he lost the glasses my mother made him get in order to be able to read any print smaller than headlines. He squints at a few pages, pauses at those which have the hymns printed on them to read the titles that are printed in the large, Old English Text font of the Lutheran hymnal he's sung from for more than eighty years. Finally, he closes his eyes, one hand resting across a page, and begins to sing "The Old Rugged Cross."

I take my father to dinner, eating in a restaurant so familiar he can order what he's had three times before without having to read the menu. On the way back to his house he asks me to park on Butler Street for the first time in nearly twenty years. The street is so deserted, there is room for ten cars, but I know to drift up to where a vacant lot sits among the buildings that house bars, a beauty shop, a tattoo parlor, and a long-closed hardware store that still sports its name on the side of the building. He uses his cane to shuffle into the middle of that empty space where the bakery he owned for sixteen years used to stand.

"The bakery's been missing so long, pretty soon no one will know it was here," he says.

---

1. I originally came upon some of the odd histories in *Elephants on Acid and Other Bizarre Experiments* by Alex Boese

"Probably," I say, an easy agreement. It's been almost forty years since the building was torn down a few months after the bakery closed. Shortly afterward, the cement we're standing on was laid over the vacant space to provide parking for people who rented the rooms above those nearby businesses, though now, when I glance up, I can't see any lights in the upstairs rooms on either side of us and no cars are parked near where we stand.

I half expect him to begin a hymn, but instead he leans on his cane and says, "The house where I was born is gone, and the house where you were born is gone," sounding so mournful I offer to drive him to both sites, one leveled to make room for a widened highway, the other long ago razed and replaced by a church. With the sound of traffic passing, he seems to hear nothing of what I say.

"Right here," he says, and when he spreads his arms, I guess that he's standing at the memory of work-bench, that when he pulls his hands back together and lifts them, the cane dangling from his right hand, he is ready to carry something to the bank of ovens in the nearby remembered room.

After a few seconds he lowers his hands, steadies himself, and asks me to stand closer. He tells me my mother is slicing bread, the cash register behind her, the three of us working together because he is icing a wedding cake just before delivery, spiraling sweetness so thick with sugar and lard around the figures of the bride and groom, no one should eat it, trusting me to balance the three white tiers to the car.

7

After my student tells me about her lost twin, I read that before the use of ultrasound, the diagnosis of the death of a twin or multiple was made through an examination of the placenta after delivery. Now, with the availability of early ultrasounds, the presence of twins or multiple fetuses can be detected during the first trimester. A follow-up ultrasound would reveal the "disappearance" of a twin.

8

The year my father turns eighty-nine, a scientist suggested that the new superconductor was capable of creating a cosmological bomb billions of times more powerful than the atomic bomb. He said the odds were as likely as one chance in ten, at least one chance in fifty, speaking like a bookie about the end of Earth when the superconductor began to operate at full power. The rest of his scare was an explanation of how showers of heavy-mass particles might end us with ultra-dense quark matter, the vocabulary for our vanishing full of unrecognizable nouns.

I wanted to dismiss it, but during the week in which I read that scientist's warning, two friends my age died on successive days, and I woke on the third to a phone call I believed was one more, as if a chain reaction had begun, as likely, it seemed as the seven billion of us becoming fodder for a brand new black hole because those superconductor scientists were poised on the brink of Genesis, hurtling back to where nothing is alive but the gods.

9

Because his house becomes so dusty, especially the master bedroom where I sleep, I have an asthma attack during two consecutive visits. The next time I arrive, I tell him that I have other business the following day, that I have a reservation sixty miles away in order to be closer to my morning appointment.

And that's mostly true. I drive for an hour and stay in a motel along the highway I use to return home. It's one hour cut from the four-hour drive, and I've stayed late enough that the trip wouldn't have ended until after one a.m.

The motel room is clean and free of dust. I watch the late news and sports on the Pittsburgh channel that my father watches each night before he hobbles, bracing himself on furniture and the walls of his hall before lying down in the bed I slept in for thirteen years.

10

In the early 19th century there were scientists who demonstrated how electricity seemed to reanimate a dead body. Executed criminals were often used, their faces twitching, an eye opening, an arm or a leg jerking when a powerful battery was connected to particular muscles. There was enough publicity about these demonstrations that's it's nearly certain Mary Shelley was aware of them. Dr. Frankenstein, with the advantages of her fiction, was able to reanimate the dead, standing over the body like a glorious thunderhead, in love with choice.

11

Once a month, from when I was nine until I was sixteen, my father showed slides, projecting them onto the living room wall. He showed the new ones first: landscapes taken from mountain tops; old buildings shot from such a distance that my sister, my mother, and I were barely recognizable standing in front of them; close-ups of flowers he identified, walking up to the image to point out their characteristics with his finger; aging relatives we visited on vacation trips, sleeping in their houses to avoid motel bills. After that he showed old slides, all of them snapped one-by-one into the metal frames required by the projector. There was never a night when some appeared upside down. Or when a slide jammed, the wall going a brilliant white that made everyone blink.

When I was sixteen, my mother bought him a new carousel projector. In order to use it, he had to unsnap a thousand slides from those metal frames.

12

"I never would have thought," my father frequently said after my mother died, meaning that he would outlive her.

"I thought I'd be with Ruthy by now," he repeated once he passed seventy-five, and he described an afterlife that seemed to be so much a physical continuation, I thought he expected to play golf and tend a garden forever, having time to master the sport he'd taken up in his sixties, enjoying fresh vegetables for a billion meals. By the time he was past eighty, I suspected that he worried about finding himself revived as the decrepit man he was becoming.

13

In 1964, when I was a freshman in college, a scientist named James McConnell published the results of his experiments with flatworms. Flatworms were stupid, difficult to teach, but he'd rehearsed them until the brightest reacted to light, learning its link to a simple shock that McConnell supplied. He pulled aside the best of those slow learners and halved those pupils to see whether their heads or tails, both of which survived, could exceed the coin flip of chance. And later, when they were completely regenerated, he doubled those gifted students again into dozens of nervous worms, ones that quivered as soon as the light flashed to prophesize the imminence of pain. They were learning, it seemed, to anticipate the agony of an artificial sunrise and the relief of darkness. Finally, eager to discover whether learning could be physically passed from one generation to another, he fed those that had mastered the simple association of light with pain to those without such training. The success he began to claim was that what one worm had learned could be transferred to another by a regulated cannibalism.

Here, he declared, was the possibility of outrunning the slow meander of evolution. He saw the future of humanity in the precocious curling of worms, memory a matter of gorging to omniscience. There were people, subsequently, who dreamed of their children feeding upon them, how their fear and love and knowledge would be passed on to their children, keeping them, in one sense, alive.

14

"Pretty soon," my father began to say at eighty-five, "I'll be the only one who remembers the old days." He told me his "growing up" stories over and over until it seemed as if he was feeding me his memory. I was a willing listener. I didn't tell him that this was my version of revival, passing through the memories of future generations.

15

The things my mother wore:

Before we drove to church, white gloves that held a tissue to open the car door to keep them from being smudged. The new pair she kept in a box until the next wedding, Easter, or Christmas Eve. The two pair with three embroidered lines. The one pair with tiny, glittering appliqués.

While I walked into church with her each Sunday, not yet complaining about compulsory attendance, the black veils attached to her hats. The way she could make the veils flutter if she tilted her head and exhaled. How thin the cloth strands were, allowing her space to see the hymnal as she sang each hymn in alto's harmony as if she were in the choir.

In the years before illness took the weight off her body, the girdles she wore with every dress. The sound of elastic being tugged down at the end of each Sunday. How she exhaled behind her closed bedroom door.

16

Vanishing twins may occur in as many as one of every eight multifetus pregnancies and may not even be known in most cases. In one study, only three of twenty-one pairs of twins survived to term, suggesting intense fetal competition for space and nutrition. In some instances, vanishing twins leave no detectable trace at birth. More than one amniotic sac can be seen in early pregnancy. A few weeks later only one.

17

For a few years, the headless woman was a staple at the county fair. Justina, she was named one summer, and the pitch man claimed she'd lost her head in a faraway Egyptian train wreck. One year her name was Tiffany, who'd been decapitated when her speeding car ran under a truck. The last one I saw in person was Britt, the bikini girl, beheaded by a shark, so lucky, like the others, to die near a doctor who could save her.

Impossible, I said, by that time in junior high school, but just after I spoke, Britt shuddered, letting me know she was suddenly cold. "What she deserves, dressed like that," my mother observed. Britt's alien silhouette was shadowed on the wall behind us, a threat of flexible tubing twisting up like new plumbing from her sliced, scarf-covered throat.

No matter their names, by then I understood that those women's headless bodies were always going to be young and sexy, preserved for study as if research was driven by lust. The old and the heavy were left headless; nobody repaired boys who were reckless, a thing to consider. "Those women aren't angels," my mother cautioned. "Don't you forget that."

Which was fine with me. By that September, I was an eighth-grader who wouldn't admit that all I wanted was a brainless whore who knew only what touched her—my fingertips and tongue, my lips and warm breath. Right then I was wishing that if there were miracles, I'd rather have my body saved than my soul.

18

Some mornings I want to do CPR on the bodies of the exhausted words.

Nithing. Viduous. Squirk. Their denotations are so distant someone has published them to make a profit from the obsolete and rare.

Yesterday I saw marbles for sale in a museum gift shop. I plunged my hands into the bin and remembered aggies and oxbloods, cat's eyes, steelies, and glimmers, the names I've heard no one use for decades. I loitered nearby, wanting to see if even one child would choose them for souvenirs instead of a toy he could remote control. They might as well have been strands of hair plucked from the saints of our least urgent needs.

I watched while the ancient words of trespasses and hallowed came back, followed by remembering that my mother kept my first clipped hair and fingernails, that she told me I could have them some day when she was gone, though more than twenty years after her death, those things are as lost as the ancient words for *miserly person, empty,* and *embrace.*

19

At eighty-nine, my father gives up his cane for a walker. Because he is embarrassed by his weakness, I have to convince him to go to the familiar restaurant. I park by the front door and leave the car running while I help him stand. I unfold the walker and set it up for him, telling him to go inside while I park the car.

When I return, he hasn't moved. During dinner he says, without any prompting, "When you have just one son, there's no room for anything terrible to happen."

20

I mention to the student who absorbed her twin that my daughter sent me ultrasound photos of both of her yet-to-be-born. That I stuck those photos among cards and snapshots and short lists of things-to-do on my refrigerator, not telling her my daughter asked not to know their sex, her two daughters old enough, now, to study their early selves like scholars of pre-birth.

21

Things my mother used:

Two stationary tubs in which she moved the laundry from side to side, rinsing until she lifted each item and guided it into the wringer, the tight space between the rollers squeezing the water from our clothes, preparing them for the light

The clothesline woven between two steel clothes posts cemented into the back yard. Dozens of wooden clothespins to suspend our laundry above the small lawn through the afternoon from March to November, above the cement cellar floor in winter, where they hung for two or three days like ghosts of ourselves.

Her flat iron. The water she sprinkled to keep its heat from scorching, pressing everything, even our underwear, before she let it retouch our bodies.

22

My daughter has painted a sky of chairs that sparkle like redundant constellations. Her heaven is moonless, the chairs, she says, ascending. The sky bleeds from one side from the wounds she imagines on an adjacent panel, one that waits nearby, brilliant with light. Her two daughters, ages seven and four, dream of painting it blue, a sun shining the chairs invisible.

23

Things my mother did for my father:

Turned on the television. Changed the channel and adjusted the rabbit ears until he could make out the Pittsburgh Pirates or a football game.

Let him read the newspaper at the dinner table, the sports section spread out by his plate while she talked to my sister and me through dinner as if we were a family of three.

Dialed the black, rotary phone in the kitchen. Called him when the person he wanted to speak to answered.

24

When my mother died, my father called no one for months, complaining that "Everyone has forgotten me."

25

On the way to visit my father, I pass the former site of West View Amusement Park, gone more than thirty years into apartments, a grocery store, the fast foods of familiar franchises. I park where the roller coaster turned sharply before it reached the road and West View's business district. When I close my eyes for a minute to imagine the park restored, one passer-by raps on the window to ask if I need help.

26

The science of the three-moon era:

The enormous impact that spawned our moon could have sent other satellites into orbit as well. They likely remained in their orbits for up to 100 million years. Then, gravitational tugs from the planets would have triggered changes in the Earth's orbit, ultimately causing the moons to become unmoored and drift away or crash into the Moon or Earth. The tugs from the other planets are very, very tiny, but they changed the shape of Earth's orbit, which changed the effect that the Sun's gravity has on the moons, which destabilized the lost moons.

27

Things my mother left behind:

Four black veils attached to hats stored in a box under a thick comforter high on the steps to the attic. Five pair of white gloves, two pair in boxes, unused.

Deep in a drawer of lingerie, two girdles untouched for a decade

A washing machine with a wringer attached. A hundred feet of clothes line. Eighty-seven wooden clothes pins. A flat iron. The glass bottle with a sprinkler's head on top. The bottle clear, the head light green.

28

There is a haunting poem by W.S. Merwin called "For the Anniversary of my Death." It begins, "Every year without knowing it, I have passed the day / when the last fires will wave to me." Anyone reading those lines surely considers the anniversary of his own extinction.

It's less stressful to research the date and place some species we've never seen died for good—the final great auk on Elday Island, the last Labrador duck outside New York.

Even more exact, the ones exhibited like the lone Carolina parakeet that collapsed on February 21st, 1918, at the Cincinnati Zoo. The final dusky seaside sparrow dying on display inside DisneyWorld, June 18th, 1987, those one-of-a-kinds living for months or years without seeing a body like their own. The rest of us moving on without them, the world made irrefutably new by one more emptiness.

29

Simultaneously, during the three-moon era:

The crescent moon of anticipation,
The half-moon of mercy,
The full moon of joy.

30

When my wife and I are dressed and healthy, her body temperature registers eight-tenths of a degree colder than my ordinary one of 98.6.

She shivers in any weather below seventy degrees. Occasionally, in Central Pennsylvania, she wears gloves in May and September. It's not much good joking about how she's farther from fever, how sweaters become her, how her jackets are stylish and smart. Or, if I feel the need to use a bit of trivia I picked up from the local PBS station during half time of a football game, to bring up the Thomsonians, who believed all sickness was caused by a deficiency in body heat, claiming that every disease could be cured by a medicinal steam bath.

It's something to consider because three months past ninety, my father is wrapped in two late August sweaters, the furnace growling in his delirious house where each plant has wilted like his short-term memory and his stove, for the past year, has been covered by signs that say *NO* in large letters to lower the probability for fire. My wife and I have driven the 200 miles to Pittsburgh the day after our own discussion of aging, meeting with a woman who specializes in Elder Law, the legalese of wills and trusts for the future distribution of whatever assets we have, the talk turning to assisted living, comas, and long-term vegetative states while air conditioning chilled my wife to putting on the jacket she carries, even in the heart of summer, for overcooled rooms.

Afterward, walking outside to the surprise of warmth, she didn't remove her jacket. "How could you stand it?" she said.

"She made everything seem hypothetical," I said. "It was like we were talking about somebody else who was going to fall apart and die."

My wife hugged herself in the late afternoon sun. "I mean the cold," she said. "It was absolutely freezing in there."

31

Within one of those annotated lists featuring "famous last words" is the final one spoken by Dr. Joseph Green, a nineteenth-century English surgeon. Upon taking his own pulse, he managed, according to *The New Book of Lists*, to say "Stopped" before he died.

My father, by the end of September, has been moved to a facility for the nearly dead. He has a room with a door that doesn't lock, and the first time my wife and I visit he is wrapped in a flannel shirt and one of those sweaters from August, both buttoned to his throat while the heat hums from three baseboards on a warm fall afternoon.

My wife places her jacket on a chair. My father, nearly deaf, guesses at what we say. "That's good," he comments from time to time, imagining, I'm nearly certain, that we're telling him about how well we're doing or what our children have accomplished. "Nothing much going on here," he says at last, but he has begun to take his pulse every ten minutes or so as if he expects to hear, like that dying British doctor, the moment it will stop.

"Let me show you something special," I say, before I wheel him to the elevator that takes us one floor below to where I remember the chapel is located.

He doesn't react to the brief journey. My wife helps me navigate his chair between a set of pews in the chapel, and I wheel him to the window he purchased fifteen years ago, a stained-glass mural in memory of my mother who, at that time, was already more than five years dead.

Even when I set him inches from the plaque that states his name and hers, he doesn't recognize anything. I ask him to read, but despite this prompt, he doesn't seem to understand. My wife, who stands nearby, bends down and reads the words aloud, shouting into his ear.

"How about that?" my father says. "It's for Ruthy."

"Yes," I say, "you paid for it."

"How come I've never seen this?" he says, and I wish I'd brought along the photograph of him standing beside the window the day it was unveiled.

My father stares at the window for a minute, and then, without taking his eyes off it, he begins to reminisce about my long-dead mother. He settles on listing old gifts he bought for her—a set of pearl earrings, a Sunday-dress, and a piano, all of them things that my sister helped him pick out.

He doesn't mention the one time he asked me to help. In late November, for their fifteenth anniversary, the gift of wax fruit he'd somehow set his heart upon. "Each piece will last and last," is how he put it. I was eleven years old and didn't ask him to reconsider his choice. I thought the fruit looked real, the colors blended to look just short of ripe, as if, when he arranged them in the wooden bowl that sat on our kitchen table the following day, they would be perfect,

My father handled the apples and pears; he hefted the peaches, bananas, and bunched purple grapes. He seemed to be weighing them. Finally, he made a small pile of assorted wax fruit on the department store's counter top, estimating, I thought, the size of our kitchen's wooden bowl that was usually full of opened envelopes and advertising circulars that featured store coupons my mother intended to use.

The next afternoon, while my mother was changing clothes after church, he dumped all of the paper out of the bowl and placed the mess on the dining room table. With his right hand, he swept his breakfast sweet roll crumbs into his left and shook them into the wastebasket. He ran hot water into the stained coffee mug he used for a week between washings, a habit, he'd told me once, that he believed was his gift to my mother because reusing it reduced the number of dishes she had to scrub every day.

Finally, he spread that wax fruit out like a set of trophies. The grapes were the last to go into the arrangement, lying on top, the overhead light reflecting off their surfaces. "Isn't this a pretty picture?" he said when he'd finished. I heard my mother coming down the hall. Before she entered the kitchen, he added, "Just think. They'll look beautiful forever."

32

The vanished twin can die from a poorly implanted placenta, a developmental anomaly that causes major organs to fail or to be completely missing, or there may be a chromosome abnormality incompatible with life.

33

For a year or two, just after that wax fruit anniversary, I was fascinated by pretending to be dead. "Soon enough, your time will come," my mother said, catching me holding my breath in front of the sweep hand for seconds on my bedroom clock radio. "Kid stuff," she said. "You should know better."

After that, I was more careful about my secret pastime, one that moved past simple breath-holding. In a library book, I studied what the mystics did to appear as if they'd stopped their hearts, shutting down the pulse with a block of wood under the armpit, pressure that worked like a tourniquet. I kept the book in my desk at school, but I mastered that technique well enough to simulate a stilled heart. I laid fingers to my wrist as I died, coming back again and again to briefly muffling one part of my autonomic system, dying in my room, or better, among trees in the game lands near our house, lying down where somebody, some day, might discover me. I stared at the path I'd taken to whatever small clearing I'd chosen, imagining hikers who would turn curious or eager or absolutely afraid, everything so still for seconds that I believed in the power of leaving and returning, the comfort of being sprawled like the nearly drowned, doing CPR on the self, taking that first great gasp and bringing my heart's beat back after someone laid fingertips to my wrist, holding them there in wonder.

34

The second time my wife and I visit the nursing home, I notice that my father has no pictures of my mother in his room, which means I have two more pictures of her in my house than he displays. "Do you want a picture of Mom?" I ask, and he shakes his head.

"It won't bring her back," he says, for once not saying "That's good." I show him the wedding announcement I've discovered between the pages of a book about the national parks he had sitting out in his living room. He nods and recites all four paragraphs from the local weekly newspaper. "Thanksgiving, 1941," he says. "Dorothy Seitz, maid-of-honor. Ruth Lang, given by her brother Karl. Mildred Van Wegan (nee Lang) attended from Michigan. The Reverend Blair Claney officiated."

How many times had he read that notice in the twenty years since she'd died? "We had the long weekend for our honeymoon," he says. "And a week after that, the war."

It's nearly Halloween by now, and the children of the nursing home staff wear costumes and go from room to room to do an indoor trick or treat. My father, because he can't hear or he doesn't read the facility's weekly newsletters, doesn't understand, so he has no candy on hand. Regardless, he seems fascinated by the princesses and vampires. "Remember *Frankenstein?*" he says. "I saw it in the theater as a boy. Boris Karloff. That was scary for a boy my age. And then he was in all those movies about trying to raise the dead."

"It's a wish that's always with us," I say, but he doesn't hear.

"Remember *Frankenstein?*" he says again. "I saw it in the theater as a boy. Boris Karloff. That was scary for a boy my age. And then he was in all those movies about trying to raise the dead."

I consider showing him the wedding notice again.

Nearly twenty-one years ago, after my mother died at home, my father told me, "Your mother didn't want a hospital. She'd just seen her sister in misery with the tubes and machines and all that coming to nothing."

This week, when we talked on the phone, my sister has told me that his chart says *Resuscitate* where a choice is asked for. Thirteen years ago, nearly eight years after my mother died, my father's heart was stopped during bypass surgery. For a year, each time I visited, he showed me his scar. "The things they can do," he said. Within the next few years, his brother and sister died of cancer. "There has to be a limit on miracles," he said at the time. "Maybe it's one for each family."

When we get home, I look up Boris Karloff's films. Sure enough, there are some that sound as if they repeat the plot of a doctor trying to raise the dead. *The Man They Could Not Hang* and *The Man with Nine Lives,* for two. The plots feature grave robbing and secret serums for curing cancer and providing eternal youth. The common denominator is Boris Karloff as the mad scientist, not the reanimated body.

35

During the 1950s, a Soviet surgeon named Vladimir Demikhov sewed the heads of puppies onto full-grown dogs. Both heads were alive. The puppies even lapped milk with their tongues, though it ran from their severed throats. This is how we will be revived one day, he said, meaning with the hearts and lungs of others. Tissue rejection killed those dogs in a month or less.

Those puppies must have wondered why the milk dribbled out behind them. Their heads remind me of old dolls, the way their rubber faces, always with their one expression of breast hunger, could be squeezed loose from their pink, sexless bodies.

Those full-grown dogs, on the other hand, must have been aggravated every moment by the nuisance of a second, useless head.

36

I've made a list of the times I might have died, yet, as my mother always said, "Lived to tell about it":

Pneumonia—four bouts, each one relieved by antibiotics.

Being a passenger in a car driven by drunks or speeders—a good many times before the age of twenty-two, surviving each trip unscathed and discovering, months or years later, that several of those drivers eventually killed themselves behind the wheel.

Falling asleep while driving—not me, but the man who'd picked me up as I hitchhiked, a corn field fortunately level with the highway at the spot where he left the road.

The list doesn't seem extraordinary except for the time that I braked my Volkswagen hatchback hard when a trailer truck I was passing suddenly veered into my lane. The hatchback locked into a four-wheel drift, lurching sideways across the median strip and through two lanes of oncoming, limited-access speeding traffic, somehow missed by all of them before the tires, just as miraculously, caught on the opposite shoulder as I spun and ended up facing sideways.

I took a breath and chose a break in the traffic to cross back to my lanes, swerving into the passing lane where I'd been seconds before. Two miles later I exited and found myself behind that same truck at a stop light. The truck driver climbed down and walked toward me. It was summer. The car wasn't air conditioned. My window was open. He bent down and said, "Fuck, I'm so sorry. You must be sitting in it."

It didn't take his shaken expression to convince me I'd had something like a last-second pardon.

37

In November, I read that another new oldest living person has been certified, beginning her bout with the condensed celebrity of age. As always, the biography opens with the frequencies of cigarettes, beer, and deep-fried dinners. Nobody mentions those faraway villagers who once helped to sell yogurt based on its connection to longevity. The rustic-looking peasants in the television commercials were seen enjoying yogurt while the announcer claimed most of them were over one hundred years old and that some of them were one hundred and twenty or more.

I think of Joice Heth, the slave who nursed George Washington, yet lived to be displayed by P.T. Barnum at one hundred and sixty-one. Her secret, Barnum explained, was thinness, just forty-six pounds on her ancient frame, as if fasting, not yogurt, was the best defense against death.

My father is approaching half his former weight of 210 pounds. No matter what's served, he cleans his plate; he craves a nightly snack. He hoards the cookies and candy he refused for more than eighty years, making himself sick with overeating in his nursing home room. "Like a little boy," he says, and then he weeps.

He tells me the woman two rooms away, just turned one hundred and one, barely leaves her bed, her bald scalp shimmering pink as a wound. "Ten more years of this," he says, "imagine," the future palpable enough to flop belly-first across his bed, the mattress sighing while the well-fed constellation of inevitability blinks on above the horizon, dragging the dark by its hair, shoulders bent against the weight.

I turn on the television and find a football game, but he slumps forward in his wheelchair, staring at a spot on the carpet between his feet. It's no wonder the shrieks of Earth, as scientists say, can be heard from space, such collective terror slithering along our tongues as we struggle to recall even the wrong answers that blink, strobe-like, in the brain until we nearly choke on confusion, our mistaken guesses speeding skyward, humming like the panicked prayers of the dying.

And now, after more than eight decades of devotion to his church, he says nothing about eternal life, not even the back-lot pearly gates set piece of childhood. He says less and less, his sentences shrinking like cheap trousers until, during this visit, we share the long conversation of the unsaid, rehearsing the future.

38

Sometimes there are verifiable revivals. It has been confirmed, for example, that a man in Chile woke in his coffin. Sitting up, dressed in his finest suit, he asked for a drink of water before rejoining his family.

Sometimes, however, one revival comes carrying the direct consequence of loss: My student, years ago, was tagged incorrectly after an auto accident, his parents discovering the dead body of his friend when they were asked to verify his identity. Eventually, they were escorted to a private room so that the parents of the other young man, just arriving with anxiety and joy, would not cross their path. "Inconceivable" was how a colleague put it when we heard how they had to be told that a mistake had been made, the mother and father guided, at last, to confirm what everyone now understood to be the truth.

And sometimes revival can be extraordinarily terrible: Primo Levi relates that during his days in a Nazi concentration camp, he was assigned to dispose of bodies after a gassing. On one of those occasions, a girl rose from the dead tangle of the gassed, and his work crew was saddened past despair because there was never charity in the camp, all of them knowing she would be returned to the gas, unbearably understanding what was coming, her resurrection so dreadful it would madden the living.

39

Some animals have returned from the dead, resurrected after a century extinct like the Cebu Flowerpecker or Jordan's Courser, both of them sighted and confirmed by the radar of science.

It's the work of Thomas, such confirmations, as close as laying fingertips to wounds. Consider the naturalist on Fiji who searched for Macgillivray's Petrel.

His optimism as he set out to lure the lost from extinction's deep privacy. He spent a year sounding its call like a prayer against absence until one morning the long-missing bird flew into his head as if he were the object of desire.

Consider, too, how to present that news, breathlessly beginning, "Listen." What's next to say? Each thick history of belief is crammed with illustrations that depict the loneliness of the single sighting, the man, recently, who claimed he had seen the Ivory-Billed Woodpecker sixty years after its case was closed tight by science. Without corroboration, he's become the prophet for improbability, someone with a camera who sits still and loves the silence of expectation while every faint flutter of color turns into the promise that phantoms whisper.

40

My wife and I visit my father a few days before Christmas. He nods off at short intervals, a signal, I'm sure, that something serious is decreasing the amount of oxygen that is reaching his brain. During the four hours we are there, the only thing he responds to is an old album of photos. "Everybody in here is dead," he says, able to name his sister and his three brothers, his two best friends, and three girlfriends, one of whom, near the end of the album, is my mother. His head sinks, one hand resting on her picture. I measure his breathing until he snaps back.

I talk to him by phone on Christmas, calling when I know my sister is there so she will answer and tell him it's me. Twice, as we speak, I am sure he nods off because there is more than a minute without a response, not even a "That's good." Two days later, while I'm interviewing candidates in San Francisco for a position at my university, he dies.

His minister tells me that my father has fallen back into resurrection's arms, his body surrendering its balance to the trust exam of eternity. He is intent on convincing me that all's well, that the dead are always revived. He doesn't ask me if I share that faith.

41

Some scientists speculate that small, asteroid-sized objects would have lasted the longest as the lost satellites. "They would have looked more like Jupiter or Venus in the sky than a satellite," one scientist has said. "They would have resembled very bright stars."

42

After all the post-funeral things are settled, I make two last visits to my father's house, keeping them as short as possible, the asthma attack-inducing dust an issue, now, in every room. What I want most are photographs, especially those that help to deny the *never* of what is irretrievable.

I spend half of that time in my old room rummaging in boxes from department stores that closed decades ago. Inside one from Horne's are photos so unfamiliar that I barely recognize myself from ages six to eleven. After I look at others in the box I can tell that the photographs were taken by an uncle, that they were stored in my bedroom closet after both he and my aunt had died. My father, about ten years earlier, had claimed all of them from another empty house.

My sister, a church choir director, keeps the book of hymns.

43

The moon, recently, was a celebrity, full and a few miles closer than usual, enough to bring two neighbors outside near midnight. A perigree moon, science calls it, the tides heaving up higher as well. Looking at his watch, one of my neighbors suggested "Auld Lang Syne," but I was alone with remembering the approach of planet Melancholia in a film I had seen the year before, how, for one perfect night, it was sized exactly like the moon, the sky brilliant with the fascination of malevolence and the approach of oblivion.

44

Today I woke with the coffee maker set to six a.m., its cough driving me out of sleep like a smoke alarm. Within an hour, three birds flew into the living room windows, one of them dead in the iris, the other two missing. A neighbor says it's three flights of the same bird, but I remember the music of those thumps, the variation of size and speed, and I see the colors of the vanished above the trees, shades necessary as water as I stand beneath them, my face upturned to spaces they have left in the sky.

PITTSBURGH

Recognition

During the tour of a history of psychiatry museum, our group pauses before a children's chair exhibit, what seems little more than a large, clumsy box. To illuminate its purpose, there are photographs taken during its "in-use days" in the lunatic room of a hospital. The photographs are dated recently enough to include my childhood. The guide, a college student, says the chair had sufficient size to enclose the legs of even the largest child. "For instance," she says, "notice the door's double padlock," and points below where the patient in that photograph sits straight-jacketed, face obscured by the stiff mesh spit and bite shield. "The child is there for a reason," she says. "Disobedience, most likely. Or behavioral outbursts." It seems an illustration of "never" or "impossible."

When I was young, it was not uncommon for those who cared for me to threaten a straight-jacket when they disapproved of my behavior. From our car, one day, my mother identified a large building we were passing as an asylum. Tired of my "acting a fool," she said, "A wing is reserved there for children."

Some teachers said, "If you can't sit still or stay quiet, then ..." and nearly always we did, not talking back, not moving or cursing or calling out awful names. What were our classroom crimes but "disobedience"? What provoked my parents and relatives to threaten with the nut house and the loony bin but "behavioral outbursts"? Such quiet I kept at school and at home. Acquiescence.

Once, a boy two years younger than I was moved into my friend's house. "A foster child," my mother said. "Go and meet him." And for half an hour, the three of us played in my friend's living room. When some small toy became important for both of them to hold, that foster child, without speaking, lifted a heavy glass ashtray from the coffee table and swung it so hard into my friend's skull I thought he'd killed him. I heard myself scream from somewhere far away while that boy bit his own arm hard enough to draw blood. I understood he meant that wound to justify self-defense, that my unconscious friend would need to graft whatever he remembered onto the story I'd tell.

And then that foster child waited. My friend stirred. His mother didn't ask anything of me except to "leave this minute." Before the day ended, that boy was, as my mother reported, "back in the system." Nothing else was said. The spare room in my friend's house retrieved its sewing machine and ironing board, the space, his mother said, "useful again."

I am saying "boy" because I forgot his name, though that summer before fourth grade, for my mother's joy, I recited the names of everyone who lived in the eleven houses on our street, and even now I can recall enough of them to ace the simple SATs of nostalgia, yet settling on calling him "that foster child" the way I sometimes say, "Here, boy" to a stranger's dog, expecting it to be pleased by what passes for recognition.

Solitude

Sixth grade was a year of waiting alone at the school bus stop like a runaway who might welcome the car of a stranger. Twice, snow swirling, men offered rides. And once, in good weather, I shook my head, afraid to reveal my high-pitched, obedient voice. Mostly, I sang radio hits like "Don't" and "You Send Me" half aloud, but after the last day, dismissed at noon, I forgot my glasses in their brown case I'd opened only for black board quiz emergencies. My mother drove me the four miles to where they lay inside the desk no longer mine.

Building cleared, I thought, I wove in and out of every upstairs room, grades three through six. I sat in each teacher's padded chair and knew I wouldn't recognize anyone in the farthest seats. For three years, I had hardly worn my glasses, but suddenly I put them on and wore them downstairs where, in the second-grade room, the teachers were sitting around a table, their lunches spread on wax paper and flowered napkins. Two were smoking, and when one laughed, she was a stranger who called to me, asking why I had returned, a question I answered with the truth, wondering if anyone around that table had recognized me.

In three months, nine schools like that one emptied into a building that housed students who drove cars and drank beer and fucked each other. I walked to a bus stop where eleven of them bunched, all two or more years older. I carried my glasses like a wallet from room to room eight times each day and learned to behave like I didn't know how small I could become. And though I understood the risk, I sought rides that year, not wearing the glasses, not once bringing them with me when I walked backward to face traffic, thumb extended, and climbed into every car that stopped because I needed to cover five miles to where boys I wanted as friends lived in houses I could see were better than mine, their landscaped yards walking distance from that crowded, consolidated school.

Each Saturday, my mother was busy with work from six to six; my father slept after twelve hours of night shift, and half of the dashboards displayed St. Christopher, the other half bare or wrapper-littered. Women drove immaculate cars that smelled like cigarettes, their eyes leaving the road each time they talked; the men stared straight ahead, and yet seven suggested I might share their desires, not ashamed to describe them aloud, all seven asking again, three offering cash while I concentrated on the passing fog of landscape as if I could recognize anything more than a few feet from where I squinted, learning the demands of loneliness and longing.

Weekend

After seventh grade basketball practice, you ride the late-bus, a trip that lasts half an hour before it reaches your stop that is still nearly two miles from your house, hitchhike distance, but less than half a mile from your parents' bakery. Because it's Friday, you're supposed to go there to help your mother close the shop.

It's 5:30 when you walk inside. Your mother is sweeping the floor behind the counters near the bread slicer. You drop your gym bag and your physical science book on one of the two chairs that sit on either side of the hardworking space heater. "Keep watch," your mother says. "Call if somebody comes in."

Hardly any customers show up this close to closing. The nearby mill that is rumored to be closing has a shift that ends at three. To ease rush hour traffic exiting nearby Pittsburgh, parking is forbidden between four and six. But the pans are always there to scrub, the emptied display ones as well as the heat-darkened ones used for baking. On Fridays, sales are higher and more pans are emptied. Tonight, baking begins four hours earlier than Monday through Thursday. Saturday is the busiest day of the week by far, the "make or break day" according to your mother.

Your mother scalds bakery pans in an ancient sink that sits in the back corner of the preparation room. She never wears the "housewife-tested" rubber gloves modeled on television. She never passes her hand under the open faucet to feel for temperature, trusting steam to mean there is heat enough to scrub the sugar left by sweet rolls and doughnuts, by coffee cakes and pies, flat pans sanitized and glistening on edge, reflecting the sunset's last light just before she switches to the deep pans for baking pecan rolls and upside-down cakes, fruit and nuts scattered over the greased bottoms so the cakes lift out gleaming with sweetness.

Two customers come in. One buys a loaf of day-old bread for half price. The other chooses the last seven cherry-filled sweet rolls, and your mother, because it is late, charges her the price for half a dozen.

Outside, it is midwinter dark by six. Your sister, who is fourteen, will have dinner made, but your half hour in the bakery is only a preliminary.

Since seventh grade began, Friday nights mean working beside your father for three hours and earning a dollar an hour. Shortly after seven, your mother drops you and your father off in front of the bakery and drives to her mother's house. She will peel apples there and slice them for your father to scatter on tomorrow's coffee cakes. It is only a mile. Her sister lives there too, and they can "catch up" for a few hours.

You grease pans and weigh dough to place in pans that shape bread. You measure ingredients. You punch the next batch of rising dough and leave it under a cloth cover to rise again. You stand for three hours in the unheated room that has no foundation beneath it. The low ceiling captures heat from the adjoining room's ovens so that your face roasts while your feet freeze until your mother returns shortly after ten to drop off the sliced apples and drive you home.

You stay up past midnight to watch *Chiller Theater*. Saturday is the one day to sleep in, and you are in love with monster movies. When you sit on the floor about six feet from the screen, your mother says, "Don't sit so close." You slide back a few inches and wait for her to walk down the hall to her room. You are three years from contact lenses. The new glasses that you wear for blackboard work are in your school locker. When you move close to turn down the volume because she never closes her door, you barely move back at all, sitting twice as close as before. Body snatchers, mummies, and werewolves are exciting, but what you like best are the vampires because they always seem to find women in negligees and sexy dresses to attack. You are twelve and obsessed with breasts. For now, you have settled for making a pledge to yourself to kiss a girl before the school year ends.

Your mother expects your door to stay open all night, but you never hear her leave in the morning at 5:45. Around nine, you hear your father come home. He will get up before three to take your older sister to the bakery to help out, but when you walk into the kitchen, he eats breakfast with you before he goes to sleep.

By ten o'clock, you are hitchhiking to Mt. Royal Boulevard where the friends you've made this year all seem to live in house set on quiet streets a block or two from the boulevard. Since you started working on Fridays, your parents have allowed you to thumb rides as long as they are "local." You will never mention the woman who smoked and slurred her words when she picked you up. You will say nothing about the man who asked if you had a girlfriend, who, when you said "no," asked, "Do you ever play with your friends, you know? Good-looking boys like you should enjoy themselves or let someone do it for them."

You have to be home by five so you can ride back to the bakery with your father. Your mother is washing pans again; your sister is waiting on customers. Your job is to tend a fire that burns a week's worth of cardboard and paper in a depression behind the bakery. In January, even near the fire, you are never warm enough because you refuse to wear a hat or earmuffs, even where there is no chance some classmate will see you.

Your mother makes dinner and serves it at seven. Meat, potatoes, and a vegetable like always. Pizza is unheard of; sandwiches aren't dinner. She washes the dishes by hand, scalding smears of grease before arranging the plates and silver in rubber slots for drying.

You shower and dress and watch a few minutes of Dick Clark's weekly rock and roll show before she drives you to the high school for the junior high winter social. After half an hour of excuses and delays, you dance with a girl who some other girl says, "Likes you." Encouraged, you stay on the gym floor with her after the song is over. The second-hand information seems to be true. For the rest of the dance, you think that maybe this is the night that first kiss occurs,

You stay behind to talk with her in the school lobby, but two of her friends stand close by, one of them saying, "Come on, my brother's outside, and he has his girlfriend with him, so you know he's in a hurry to dump us."

Though you are only ten minutes late coming outside, your mother is angry. "Where have you been? It's late," she says.

"I was talking to Nancy Jenkins," you say, and she looks at the three girls who are coming down the stairs.

"They all look like they live out the boulevard," she says.

"They do," you say.

"You be careful. Watch your manners." She doesn't ask which of the girls is Nancy Jenkins.

Your mother says nothing else during the five-mile drive. There is no radio in the station wagon. She follows the boulevard for a half a mile before she turns down the hill toward the highway that is lined with factories and businesses, turning again at the strip mall and trailer court before she drives up the hill where your house sits among others that are small but mostly well kept.

In the driveway, she turns off the engine and says, "I'm glad you had fun, but I have a terrible headache, and there's church in the morning, so no *Hit Parade* for me tonight. Anyway, I bet your father turned off the TV. Ever since *Gunsmoke* chased George Gobel away, he gets up and makes himself a sandwich at ten o'clock."

Your sister is in her room studying on a Saturday, but sure enough, your father is at the kitchen table as if he'd positioned himself to make her look like a fortune teller. Despite her headache, your mother turns on *Your Hit Parade*. Half an hour later, the #1 song turns out to be "April Love."

"I'm glad a nice song like this is still number one," your mother says. "I think poor Snooky Lanson left the show because he had so much trouble with those Elvis songs. It's way easier to be Pat Boone."

So easy, you want to say, that Dorothy Collins is singing "April Love" tonight. As if your father agrees, he stands in the kitchen doorway and begins to sing along, except he belts out the words at his own pace, smudging what Dorothy Collins is crooning while you watch her breasts lift when she reaches her arms toward a shadow that suggests her distant lover.

When your father shows no sign of shutting up, what you notice is not how exhausted your mother looks, but how she bites her lip throughout the song as if she wants to scream at him for ruining the performance. You realize there is nothing about the way his voice sounds that would shape the sounds into a chorus that deepened the emotion for any listener, but when your mother stands, catching herself on the arm of the couch, you wish your father would take her hand and dance or at least shut up and hug her, but he keeps singing the last chorus out of sync while she walks down the hall to leave Saturday behind.

In the morning, your mother has eggs ready with the coffee cake that didn't sell yesterday. It's slathered with maple icing, and you tell yourself that it's no wonder it was ignored by customers. "How come the fresh apple ones are never left over?" you say.

Your mother says, "Only the early birds get those."

"They're the best," you say, and she gives you a smile that already looks tired before she stands behind you, places her hands on your shoulders, and squeezes, saying, "Thank you for that," and you try to say something wonderful and manage "You're welcome."

In church, off to the side in the front row, you sit with three friends. All of you are acolytes, but this isn't your Sunday to wear the embarrassing white smock and light candles. As you've been doing for months, you write the times each of you guess for how long the sermon will last on the back of the church bulletin. The guesses, by the rules all of you agreed to, have to be fifteen seconds apart, and today they range from fourteen to seventeen minutes. You pick fifteen-thirty, but the sermon is only fourteen minutes and twenty seconds, and you remember, too late, it's a communion Sunday when the sermon is always shorter.

None of you are old enough to take communion, that ritual a year away. Your parents and sister all sing in the choir, and they walk down with the others from the loft behind the altar to accept the wafer and the wine. As your mother turns to leave, you notice that she lays a hand on the arm of the woman beside her as if she's been surprised by a moment of unsteadiness or by a spasm of the back pain she complains about some mornings while she hovers over your school day breakfast.

As soon as you get home, your mother goes into her room to lie down. Your sister heats up leftovers for lunch while you read the sports section of the *Pittsburgh Press*. For three hours, with your bedroom door closed, you listen to the new Top 40 countdown on your small clock radio.

For once, you have sandwiches for dinner, cold cuts and cheese your father lays out with sliced tomatoes and lettuce and onions. "Your mother doesn't feel good," he says, but she comes out and sits to nibble on a piece of cheese and a handful of potato chips before she takes the section of the paper with the big Sunday crossword puzzle, the one that seems impossible to finish, into her room.

Before you finish eating, a car horn sounds from the driveway, and your sister rushes off to practice for the church pageant. You watch Ed Sullivan with your father, but when you realize there are no rock and roll singers this week, you decide to listen to the radio again. Your mother's door is open, and she looks as if she's asleep with the lights on, the puzzle lying on the floor. You tiptoe in and pick it up. There are only seven spaces left unfilled. Two of the incomplete answers are French words; two are last names of historical figures. You think of surprising her by finding the answers in your sister's French book and the cheap encyclopedia she bought through a grocery store promotion three years ago, but you know she would be angry that you cheated.

When she opens her eyes and sees you there, she says, "Turn off the light for me, would you? And leave the puzzle where you found it. I still have some work to do on it when I get a chance."

The bakery is closed on Monday, so tomorrow is laundry day. What she will do, the weekend over, you and your sister back in school, your father still asleep. Since it is January, she will feed soaking clothes through the wringer that squeezes everything as flat as cartoon victims before she hangs each item on a maze of clotheslines in the cellar and reminds everyone that "downstairs is off limits."

For the first time ever, you clear the kitchen table, run hot water in the sink, add soap and wash all of the Sunday dishes. You dry them, put them away in their proper places, and think you are learning something, that what people call their jobs is not the hardest thing they do, that whether it is out of love or resignation or some combination difficult to measure, waiting and serving are the work that never stops.

No Reason

Fifteen, I asked my friend why he needed, after lunch, to fight Art Kochanoswki, school record-holder for bench press, dead lift, and the number of suspensions in one school year. "No reason," Rich Wilson said, not pausing while we walked to the second-floor boys' room where Art Kochanowski locked the door behind the two of us and his younger brother.

Rich and Art unbuttoned their shirts and slipped out of them. Like best men, Art's brother and I folded those shirts and held them. We sized each other up, but we didn't say a word. Neither did Rich and Art. Silently, then, they fought for no reason. They swung hard, intending to harm. They grunted, stood toe-to-toe, and kept their feet. Rich Wilson's blood dripped from his nose; Art Kochanowski, though not bleeding, showed swelling below one narrowing eye

I counted the tugs on the bathroom door to seven and the knocks to ten, but it took my friend falling against a sink to end it and make me think of choices I had before Rich Wilson's jaw or ribs could be crushed by the weaponry of Art Kochanowski's boots. "Move," I said to myself, knowing the reason, but then Art Kochanowski knelt and lifted Rich Wilson's head from the floor. He whispered him back from blackout.

Rich Wilson sat up as Art Kochanowski steadied him with words his brother and I could not hear. The eleventh knock had a teacher's voice attached, but they washed their hands and faces in that stained sink as if they didn't hear "What's going on?" repeated until it became a threat. In a minute, a janitor would bring a master key, but Art's brother and I unfolded those shirts and held them up like valets. Rich and Art buttoned and tucked them into their jeans before they combed their hair. Art Kochanowski, who would lose a leg to gangrene within a year, shook my hand as if I deserved something for standing so close to danger, and then we unlocked that door, walking out in pairs, Rich Wilson and I in front because we knew we were the boys who would be trusted when we lied, our story so full of innocence we could ride that road right through the landscape of jagged questions, even keeping the Kochanowskis blameless, saying there was "No reason" the door was locked until it was true.

Faith

As late as 1892, in Vermont, the body of Mercy Brown, thought to be a vampire, was exhumed for public autopsy.
—The Smithsonian

Mercy's Father

This story begins once upon a dark, ignorant time, an age seductive with unhappiness as if ruin were a handsome prince. A father watches his neighbors pry his daughter out of her months-old grave because they believe, if her heart is uncorrupted, she is a vampire who can harm the living. And yes, Mercy's heart still bleeds. And what's more, the townspeople have faith that such a heart, in ashes, will cure consumption, burning it solving two problems. Moreover, Mercy's father and everyone there know that his son Edwin has a persistent, bloody cough, one that demands he swallow.

The Etymology of Faith

From the Latin *fidere* (11th c.), "to trust"

My Neighbor's Father

Each year, on the anniversary of its success, a neighbor's father watches a video of his heart surgery. Four years now, and because he cannot see his face or even his body beyond the cavity created for repair, it's not traumatic to see himself opened and dead, invaded by instruments. He is seventy-one and hopes to watch his heart for another twenty years. That video begins mid-operation and ends well before closing, a sampler, he says, as if his heart were one among assorted candies. "No one else has seen it but my son," he says, "and then just the once."

The Sunshine Bible Class

For adults, at the church in which I was raised, there were two Sunday school classes for what my mother called "the older crowd." Somewhere around age fifty, Sunday school attendees promoted themselves. If you were a man, you decided, one Sunday morning, to move to the Men's

Booster Class. If you were a woman, you changed rooms and settled in with the Sunshine Bible Class. Next to the afterlife, the sexes separated.

Verification

The first autopsy in the New World was performed to determine whether Siamese twins had one soul or two.

The Difficult Braille of the Body

"There's nothing to worry about," John Baird told his office boy William Taynton. Yes, but Taynton might have regretted promising, for a few shillings, to sit still in front of a hot transmitter for Baird's attempt at technological history in October, 1925. Taynton's face, if the test was successful, would be the first human's to appear on television. But didn't it say something about risk that Baird had used Stooky Bill, a ventriloquist's dummy, for his previous tests? That under all those spotlights, there was reason to imagine his soul packing to flee? Moments before, John Baird, who'd positioned him, had run from the room to see him elsewhere. Alive or dead, Taynton's face would be on television. All he had to do, the studio door closed, Baird gone to another room, was to wait and keep his faith in Baird's inarguable phrase.

The Details of the Soil

The woman who offers me clay says, "Go on," and waits as if I'm a dog sniffing at the end of a leash. The dirt eaters she grew up with are hundreds of miles from her driveway, but they've sent, for her birthday, the local clay she craves. "Go on," she advises. "Trust me. It's good for what ails you."

The Shelter Revival

After decades of disrepair, all but the crazy deserting their underground rooms, bomb shelters are back, some old missile silos refurbished by squatters who share a belief in probability. What's more, anxiety salesmen are pitching luxurious bunkers, communities for the cautious who can afford survival. Tsunami pods, tornado-proof pyramids—

shelters are versatile now, more to fear than a massive nuclear launch. They're built to endure comet strike, super volcano, solar flare, and the infinitesimal risk of brown dwarf star intrusion.

Groaning Boards

In letters to the Opinion Page of the local newspaper, the fundamentalists talk about creation, suggesting how most readers' futures are doomed to fire. They condense antiquity, squeezing out the Paleozoic, Mesozoic, and Cenozoic Eras, all that editing a means to verify Eden, claiming carbon dating one more pitchfork stab to the soul. "It's their diet," a friend says, laughing as he hands me a plate, the revivalist-picnic food line so slow I examine the broken barn across the highway, start thinking I might witness its collapse into one of those rubble piles seldom noted until someone claims its wood originally in the hands of a nineteenth-century prophet. As always, I stand in a picnic line with a plate nearly empty, searching for something to end the embarrassment of my finicky taste. The faith-healer's congregation heaps coleslaw and baked beans, meat loaf and sauerkraut, macaroni and pickled eggs, joking, "It all goes to the same place." It's the Lord's plenty while the coal trains' schedules have thinned into broth, the mines sewn back up and sealed like cancer patients. Nobody mentions subsidence, though the road to this picnic is roped by the varicose veins of tipped houses. I find applesauce and ham it takes five minutes to trim with a plastic knife before watching two old women stand and wobble and catch themselves with weight through their thighs, raising their canes and walkers like weapons.

The Etymology of Faith

The change from the Anglo-French *feid* (13th c.), "trust, confidence, pledge" to *feith* made it similar to words like truth, wealth, and health.

The Languages for Dying

Multiple myeloma, my friend says, and recites the disease chronology: chemo, thalidomide, stem cell transplant. There's Christmas still to celebrate, the days preceding it freeing me to visit where his former lover, each morning, works like a hospice aide, leaving him, this time, with a ready-to-warm lunch and laundry she has folded as tight as store displays. There are problems, he tells me, with hemoglobin, with protein numbers and platelets. He was two weeks, best guess, from kidney failure. More than a million cells, he says, two days to remove them. The treatment and replacement depleted his platelet count to three.

Verification

Not that long ago (1901), a doctor named Duncan MacDougall attempted to verify the existence of the soul by weighing the dying. He laid the bodies of those whose death was imminent on a sensitive scale. He had access. They were beyond refusing. He carefully weighed them and waited for death to weigh them again, measuring nearly one less ounce in those corpses, imagining flight as the beam dropped. Now faith was shored up by science, conversions more likely. He ran the same test on dogs, creating a control group for the soul. Waiting was the hardest part, wishing for weight loss. There were times he watched his patients' chests, sure the magic flew from the heart, a blur, MacDougall thought, when the body lightened, on average, by 21 grams. The dogs lost nothing, the air around their dying still.

My Father

Silence was my father's simple box step for avoiding the intricate dances of debate and evidence. My mother hummed a forgiveness song through her last crossword puzzle, her last letter to me, the one my father, between football games, walked to the mailbox because the forecast promised overnight snow, nodding to her his ballad of silence as her failed heart permitted the small, private grace to dress for bed before she lay down for dying. For fifty years, my father had shaken his head to dancing. He sat and waited, nervous as a patient's friend. My mother long dead, he found ways to say what cannot be said, putting on his bolo tie, polishing his shoes, and repeating, from memory, my poem about her death, reciting while I ate the breakfasts he made, sweet rolls and sausages, as if recollecting had turned so specialized he could perfect only small things. His kitchen was orange; the oven was broken; a penciled sign above it said, "Turn Off." He spoke my lines like a prerecorded message, and then he hung up, prayed, and bowed his head to eating.

Mercy's Father

This story continues with Mercy's heart on fire, with Edwin agreeing to devour its ashes, with his father looking on and listening to the sky for anything in return, with God's silence swirling the clouds as He passed over like a distant tradition.

The Etymology of Faith

From early 14th c., "assent of the mind to the truth of a statement for which there is incomplete evidence."

My Neighbor's Father

Years alone, he keeps the house exactly as it was when his wife died, but the world, he says, has learned a language he cannot translate. All morning, his small television has chanted the vowels of threat and fear. At noon, his rooms are darkened by the promise of rain. On the kitchen table, papers and books, the small, reusable place setting. The heart of a king, he's read, was mummified with mint and myrtle, frankincense and daisy. After centuries, it's a wonder that travels like a campaigner. Because, he says, they last forever, he owns a rotary phone and a typewriter. We sit only in what's left of the natural light. The rest of the day waits like a woman he's paid for.

The Sunshine Bible Class

The Sunshine Bible Class sold lilies, wreathes and seasonal greenery meant for graves. They sold maps of the Holy Land: The Sea of Galilee, the Dead Sea, the River Jordan and all the other water in dark blue while the land, by regions, was shaded in pastels like the summer dresses of women. Those maps were dotted and numbered, from one to thirty, with sites where Christ's visits and miracles took place, so those who purchased one could follow the journeys of Jesus until they seemed as simple as the mulched trails in the city park.

The Difficult Braille of the Body

There's nothing to worry about." Sure, but now it is I who hears that balloon and candy line, five fast words to reassure me, swaddled in a heavy vest, I'm safe from the side-effects of X-rays about to be rapid-fired from behind a sealed door. "There," the technician warbles, returning, "that's that," and while she undresses me I begin to tell her my favorite story from the X-Ray Chronicles: One woman sprayed herself instead of overworking the platitudes. "See?" she said, absorbing a dose, then leaning close while she shot her portfolio of bones. Three years. Four years, then the cell collapse, the technician turned into a dissolving stump of sores, Lot's wife looking forward at the towns of Regret and Death.

The Details of the Soil

"Our faith," my mother said, "begins in mud." She meant me to kneel. She meant me to pay attention to the details of the soil, acidity, depth, and texture, how likely it was to retain our region's sporadic rain.

The Shelter Revival

In school, while missile silos were being constructed throughout the country, we rote-learned every subject—state capitals, times tables, presidents and Pennsylvania counties beginning with Adams and Allegheny, where my family lived less than a mile from one site where the world would begin to end, the missiles ascending and vanishing while sirens moaned and drove us to prayer, the cover of basements, or the privacy of secret shelters where neighbors would be huddled like the eyeless, outliving us for several weeks. My father insisted we were lucky to live close to defense, those silos hidden like ancient mine shafts. He said the missiles were as reliable as crocuses, that their purple surprise would surface so quickly we would be astonished like we always were when, early in March, snow still staggering in thin flurries like residue of aftermath, those flowers, on the first bright afternoon, would rise and open, drawing us outside, our shoes churning old mulch into the dark smear of apocalypse.

Groaning Boards

Near where I live, it's God's Holiness Campground, horse and buggy, three hitching posts at the grocery, translucent skull caps on two tellers at County Trust, and one shrunken woman at this feast who's dieting a tumor away, eating dried fruit and nuts to outlive her doctor. She's up front with this year's examples; she's shaking the golf ball out of her brain. When, some nights, I dream myself dead over cliffs, beside terrorist bombs, in front of madman's shotguns, the next scene is black; I keep it to myself like fear of failure, but this afternoon insists on God as I joke with my friend who loads his plate for both of us, fat and laughing about his cabbage soup diet abandoned after diarrhea.

The Etymology of Faith

From mid to late 14th c., attached to "belief in religious matters"

The Languages for Dying

My critically ill friend once chose me to mentor him during a low-residency MFA program. Now he offers a manuscript, his portfolio of poems from a decade ago, writing, for my blessing, the history of his near transfiguration to priest. *Credo, serviam, veritas, sanctus*—each poem is titled by the Latin for formal preparation, narratives of brittle faith in the curriculum that led to the brink of ordination.

Verification

My father, once, opened a safe in his garage. Though it was simple, all of the numbers ending in zero, he had me write down the combination so that I would be sure to have access, when he died, to a coin collection, my mother's jewelry, and the savings bonds he'd purchased for my children. In 1968, Dr. Ian Stevenson suggested that the old and the dying send him combinations of locks to be opened after their deaths through friends communicating with their spirits. Immediately, he had takers, new locks carefully boxed, laid in cotton and tissue beside the names of the living who'd be willing to listen for the dead to send their combinations. Stevenson directed the aging to memorize their six numbers, giving them mnemonics for the dead: IN EDEN. HEAVEN. NO HELL. ANGELS. One hundred twenty-five thousand to one are the odds, I've been told, in that paradise lottery. This week the odds are far worse to win millions in the Pennsylvania Lottery, yet the lines to buy tickets curve through the mall. Some of the survivors gathered to listen, twirling their dials and tugging each Sargent and Greenleaf like a sword in stone, all of them losing the pick six of the afterlife.

My Father

My father's garage is hollow where his car has been gone three years, sold and replaced with the emptiness of nostalgia. Only the neighbor who has been hired to cut grass enters, raising and lowering the door from the outside. By now the face of Christ could have surfaced on the inside of that door. My father, if he returned to driving, would know miracle. My father, if he could slip his shoes on over ulcers, might reaffirm promise. His knees with no cartilage play the bone on bone etudes of pain; his pacemaker keeps one thing tuned in his body. The face of Christ could be waiting, now, for more than three years. The lawn tender could have traded my father's old tools for dope, the theft as secret as revelation.

Mercy's Father

This story ends with no change in Edwin's condition, his decline and death. Mercy's father packs his teenage daughter's things, the quilt she'd stitched from scraps and remnants to tuck under the chins of children whose hearts would have beaten in a room that shimmered like safety and longevity. Her heart of soot is so powerful, he touches her clothes, imagines her longing for a lover's breath buried between her frantic breasts that lift to his tongue and teeth as if she wished him to devour her cursed heart.

My Neighbor's Father

Listen, he says, a woman named Natalie Adler had eyes that suddenly closed and could not be opened for three days. That habit was so regular, don't you think, she could have been sent from God to remind us about how faith is tested before the re-emergence of light. He is excited about intimations of paradise, one we can believe in because it can be measured in days, because our privacies are witnessed, because our choices earn what we deserve. Think, he says, about three days of darkness that passes all understanding and thereafter lifts like eyelids.

The Sunshine Bible Class

The Sunshine Bible Class maps were as large as home-movie screens. I used to wonder where people hung them, whether they were like large tapestries in bedrooms. At a friend's house, once, I noticed one dumped in a corner of the garage among old magazines, a deflated basketball, and two headless dolls.

The Difficult Braille of the Body

"There's nothing to worry about." Maybe, but that phrase means me to think of the discomfort this procedure will save me, one more part of me repaired with the small sacrifice of minor sensitivity loss, leaving me less able to read the difficult Braille of the body. Now, the technician says, the surgeon will be back with my pictures "in a minute, just relax." On the road outside, a pair of women approach a streetlight just lit; near them, one man lights a cigarette, all three awash in superfluous light like fixed descendants of Patient Zero. Though we pass through the electric eye of fate, breaking the beam that unlocks our doors to inevitability, all of us, radiolucent, hear "There's nothing to worry about." No, though we let the invisible do its deeds, allow the CAT-scan, MRI, or X-Ray to chatter or hum or silently seethe. Though we question and are assured. Though we re-enter the dusky world, wearing the temporary confidence that has always restored us.

The Details of the Soil

I've learned there are frogs who mistake some mounds of mud for mates, and because they need to enter, they croak and squeeze, the future suddenly as irrelevant as signs of pleasure from the pliable dirt.

The Shelter Revival

In America's largest private bunker community, inside a shelter guaranteed to withstand an atomic blast, a realtor, to promote security, says the future will take us hostage, that this sanctuary for the fire next time has room enough for as many as ten, more comfortable, of course, with fewer, electricity, plumbing, and properly filtered air extra in the small town for the prepared. At ground level, the mounds are arranged as precisely as a coterie of banks, but from a distance, they are constellations, shaped by the ancient comfort of myths. The realtor evaluates like a populist who knows there is an art to survival. Soon there will be nothing but borders

Groaning Boards

When I wander, after eating, through the faithful, I recognize that some of the women who have been nodding and swaying are tied to chairs. Among these believers, I feel as if my movement could create something like an erosion gulley. A snag of guilt seems to hook my shirt from behind. I pay attention to a footfall of wind. In this grove at dusk, the old women test themselves before waiting for hands to lift them. All of the widows with humps put prayer away and limp to the taxis of their sons or nephews. They believe wings can be latent in the spine's pain, patient as wisdom teeth, as breasts or beard or birth, the rest of the body's redeemable promise.

The Etymology of Faith

Matthew Arnold, in 1873, wrote,"Faith is neither the submission of the reason, nor is it the acceptance, simply and absolutely upon testimony, of what reason cannot reach. Faith is being able to cleave to a power of goodness appealing to our higher and real self, not to our lower and apparent self."

The Languages for Dying

My friend's old lover returns like a carillon's hourly tune; the small room fills with a recessional while he talks about weight loss, confinement, the vanishing of leg strength, recovering from wheelchair to walker to cane, the black, stylish one propped against his armchair like proof of firm remission. No, he never submitted the poems, but he's signed that thesis for me, the pages worn as if turned and turned and turned, rereading the way he's repeating his latest news of plunging numbers, the apprehensive language of Revlimid, the insistence of insomnia, learning each symptom and consequence, as if, fully mastered, the future's sequence will lie unpublished.

The Details of the Soil

There was a time when frogs were thought to be generated from mud.

Verification

On television, this evening, stories of premature births, an astonishment of medical miracles, the problems that follow—children crippled, babies precarious with pneumonia, deaths of the weakest, like the son of a friend whose first son had lived a forty-hour life. He spoke for himself and his silent wife, explained complications and symptoms, the inevitability of loss. His story ended with the possibilities of heaven, how families were reunited, keeping me quiet about the woman who painted the face of a lost infant on her breast, who sat in a cabinet in the dark and waited for parents to accept the possibility of contact. Who spoke to the departed. Who bared the beautiful face of their dead child and thrust it through the shadowed, sized opening into the dim light for viewing. Who asked joyful parents to extend their hands to brush the soft faces of their children, repeating the name of the resurrected, what I couldn't do, even then, staring at the lost, cyanotic child, thinking of reassurances, the roll calls for the briefly living, what sends us back to simple light.

My Father

I sit beside my father and his elevated legs. Nothing in his living room shows a face, not my mother, nearly twenty years dead, not me or my sister or my children all of them now past, this year, the age of Christ when he preached and died. In his bedroom, his feet wrapped in gauze, my father holds out a picture of himself at eighteen, asking, "Do you believe it's me?" and because he refuses to tilt that picture up, I kneel beside his chair to say "Yes," my father keeping that picture faced my way so long, I say "Yes" again to ensure he's heard me.

The Sunshine Bible Class

After the Sunshine Bible Class was death, all of those women turning to names on the golden plaques they purchased for the church basement walls. Each year, on Pentecost Sunday, they stood to call roll from those monuments to absence, editing quietly as if they were translating the ancient stories colored into twilights, the hush we imagined in them, soft, then softer.

The Etymology of Faith

"Genuine faith is living knowledge, exact cognition, and direct experience. For many centuries people have confused faith and belief.... Faith is true knowledge and never futile beliefs." —Samael Aun Weor, *The Great Rebellion*, 2010

My Father

After his surgery, my father feels for his pulse, saying "still there" on the quarter hour like a chorus from a hymn played by the carillon from the nearby Catholic church. And though he believes his heart will soon be unnecessary in a world without gravity or sorrow, he listens and counts, gauging the tempo. Sixty-six, he says as if he's in training. Sixty-eight, stopping to expose, for the second time, his bypass scar. "Still there," he says, as if he needs to coax a heartbeat with prayer. Even when he stops watching television, when he sleeps twelve hours a day and naps three times. Even when he gives in to the walker, when he acquiesces to the wheelchair. Even when his sentences grow shorter, the ends lost like addresses, phone numbers, and names, his fingers return to his wrist for the Braille of "still there," looking down at the carpet while I wait, so quiet, holding my breath until he speaks.

Pre-Med

Whiz Kids

We were Sputnik children, the designated smart ones who had been accelerated in science and math since seventh grade, but by May,1963, we were impatient seniors bored with high school. In Southeast Asia, the United States had begun posting military advisors for a war that was so obscure none of us would ever fight, not nineteen bright boys (and two brilliant girls) taking advanced, progressive physics. Not the shortstop on our advanced physics class softball team, the Coriolis Force, who called in our scores to the *Pittsburgh Press* each time we beat the faculty, the French Club, or even the rest of the senior class minus those who played varsity baseball.

In Problems of Democracy, the map for world policies showed a large blue French Indochina where Miss Ward had hand-painted Cambodia, Laos, and Vietnam, both North and South. Maps, she said, must last ten years before replacement; this one is two years overdue, and we snickered like we had when she'd altered Africa as if countries were as temporary as high school.

What was up-to-date in our high school was physics, chemistry, biology, and math, and before 1963 ended, everyone who played for the Coriolis Force expected to be finishing his first college semester at MIT, Chicago, CalTech, or schools with less name recognition, but where, we'd been told, science flourished.

What's more, the Coriolis Force, despite a battery of eggheads, went undefeated for all nine games we played. The *Press* printed all of those scores in agate type, but by graduation all of us believed some reporter should have covered us, whiz kids who kept statistics, including batting averages taken to an extra place like the *pi* we memorized for math, science all-stars about to march off to discoveries.

Summer

In July, when I turned eighteen and had to register for the draft, a woman at a desk in Pittsburgh's Federal Building asked me for my eye color. "I don't know," I said, and instead of smiling, she glanced quickly and said "hazel," something I didn't bother to debate. I was off to college in less than two months. All I knew about a draft card was that it would admit me into the dingy, downtown Art Cinema to see movies full of naked women or to buy the raunchy magazines that were sealed in plastic on the vendor's shelves at the bus station. Drinking and voting had to wait until I was twenty-one, but Kennedy seemed like he was going to be President for another five years, and my first beer wasn't even a fantasy yet. The initial steps to medical school were on the top of my to-do list. That, and making the college basketball and tennis teams, meanwhile trying my luck with whichever girls might be interested in how I saw myself, a scholar-athlete.

All summer, my mother had headaches and what she called "the blahs." On the days when she stopped holding her head, she often carried canning jars up from the cellar. When she sat at the kitchen table, catching her breath, she sometimes snapped the ends off green beans, using that time to recover, whether the pills she took kicked in or not. Because, she explained, who else would preserve the beans or later, the tomatoes and peaches, arranging the filled, sealed jars for winter? Who else would cook and clean, strip the beds and remake them when her headaches only simmered like soup she reheated, sipping the broth because she could keep that down and work? When she stopped moaning into her pillow. When she came out of her darkened bedroom. When she could do what needed to be done. When she could save things that needed saving.

In August, Joey Reimer became the first one in our graduating class to die, driving his hand-modified old Ford off the road near our high school and into a tree. He hadn't been a whiz kid, hadn't even been going to college, but he was my age, something, my father said, to think about.

A few weeks later, during my last Friday night of working in my father's bakery from 10:30 to 5:30, my father brought up the story of the night in November, 1950, fire invaded his bakery where a tangle of wires shorted behind the ancient blue refrigerator. He explained how he had purchased the bakery earlier that year from a baker whose breath had been shortened by the invasion of emphysema. He wanted me to know that he had been lucky his lungs had stayed clear despite the clouds of flour. My father said it had taken that man a decade to die, that the baker's widow still stopped in to buy a coffee cake every Saturday.

I remembered how he had guided me, age five, through what was salvaged, and now I understood that he was trying to teach me what could be lost and the necessity of rebuilding despite everyday threats. As if he meant me to realize we were always under attack. As if he was reading my mind in order to say, at last, "Use that brain of yours if you don't want to stand on your feet all day to make a living."

First Semester

My first night at college, after enduring hours of orientation sessions, my new roommate and I piled into another freshman's beat-up Plymouth. He lived in town and wanted to drive us around to all of the places he expected to leave behind in four years. He said he knew the disc jockey who was playing rock music on the small, local station, and before we took off, he called the station from our dorm's one hallway phone and requested "Bust Out," what I told him was my current favorite song.

We drove past a factory where railroad cars were produced and one with aluminum in its company name. Except for the college, it was a Western Pennsylvania blue-collar town. The disc jockey said, "This is for the new guys at the college," and I leaned forward, ready for the aggressive guitar and saxophone instrumental I loved. Instead, I heard "Sugar Shack," a sappy, big hit for Jimmy Gilmore and the Fireballs. I was happy that he hadn't mentioned my name.

"I guess he didn't have 'Bust Out,'" my new friend said, and laughed. We drove into the country, picking up speed, but the car didn't seem to handle. "What the hell?" the driver said, and he pulled over to the shoulder. One look at the front, passenger-side tire was enough for him to say, "Whoa." The tire was tilted. He showed us how the lug nuts had come loose or had already fallen off inside the hubcap. For a few minutes, he performed only the last step of tire changing while I tried to laugh like he did.

I registered as pre-med, a first-generation college student with whiz-kid credentials of high SATs and excellent grades, placed, accordingly, in advanced math and advanced composition. All of the twenty in advanced math were freshmen; only one other was a freshman in advanced composition, a discovery I relished.

I had an eight o'clock class every day, three days in French, two in gym, where the former Marine wrestling coach lined us up and gave us the "look-to-your-left, then look-to-your-right" speech, reminding us that one out of three of us wasn't going to graduate and to think about how we could make sure we weren't among them. Terry D, a townie, was to my right. Greg L, who said he'd hated gym since junior high, was to my left. I didn't worry about my chances.

After five weeks, I hitchhiked home with a friend who lived half a dozen miles away, getting in and out of six cars to cover the eighty-five miles. The next-to-last ride was a quick eight miles with my junior high school art teacher. He remembered me because, he said, "You couldn't make yourself draw breasts on your female figures." I squirmed, red-faced.

He chuckled as he dropped us off about ten miles from where I lived. "I hope you got over that," he said. I told my friend that everybody I knew had always thought that teacher was gay.

The last ride was with a guy in his early 20s who quickly accelerated way over the backroad speed limits, cresting a hill where a cemetery entrance lay to our right. There was a line of cars turning in behind a hearse, no chance of us stopping in time. I braced myself, but that driver barely touched the brake as the line parted just enough to let us squeeze through to a variety of horn sounds. "We dodged one back there," he said, and I thought of myself as being as calm as a surgeon, outside of myself somehow rather than wallowing, like I had, in the embarrassment of awkwardly drawing a girl's body at twelve or thirteen.

The weekend was uneventful and boring. All of my whiz-kid friends were away at college. Other graduates who lived at home had jobs or girlfriends. There was nothing to do but sleepwalk through Saturday and wait for church to end on Sunday before swallowing two helpings of Sunday's roast beef dinner and riding in the rear seat as my friend's mother drove us back to school.

I tutored chemistry during the first semester. All the work felt like a rehash of what I'd learned in high school advanced chemistry. For a while I went to parties with one of my students, another freshman. She was happy with the C+ she received on the first test. "I would have failed, for sure," she said, and hugged me. I wanted to tell her I thought the hardest thing about college was getting up for my daily eight o'clock classes while my roommate slept.

But I loved advanced composition at ten a.m. I wrote and revised and wrote some more. With relish, I tackled all of the long, complicated sentences we were told to diagram. They were puzzles to solve. And their solutions filled me with a sort of academic joy.

Like times tables up to twenty, the math of each weekday's requirements was done in my head. The future wore scrubs. It washed its hands in scalding water and answered the body's questions with blades and thread.

In mid-November, I made the basketball team. Playing time was likely to be infrequent, but I had good news to take home for Thanksgiving. A week later, walking to the dorm after a Studies in the New Testament lecture, I learned that Kennedy had been shot and killed. Every station on my cheap clock radio played solemn music. The news on the television in the basement of the dorm said the country was in shock and mourning, but when I went to basketball practice, the coach ran us for the whole two hours and announced we were scrimmaging another college on Monday, what turned out to be at the same time as the funeral, Kennedy already becoming a comma in the long sentence of my first semester.

My mother, forty-three now, tried on three of my aunt's wigs before we drove off to the annual Thanksgiving dinner at my grandfather's house. She made me turn away, eyes closed, until she sported a second shade and style, asking which one I liked, whether she looked good enough to be seen in public. She was modeling like a schoolgirl, eyes meeting mine in the mirror when I stood behind her, a third wig waiting on the dresser, three styles in brown barely different under the dim overhead ceiling light, the drapes pulled shut as if our neighbors might spy her bald head. "Which one," she asked, "makes me look as if I'm alive?"

At my grandfather's, nobody seemed upset about Kennedy. I watched football with my uncles, my cousins, and my father while my aunts and mother worked in the kitchen. We were separated by the large dining room where we would finally mingle over turkey. My mother wore her wig. She acted as if she didn't mind standing on her feet for a couple of hours.

At half time, my uncles asked about pre-med. They sounded impressed. "That will be something," one of them said. "We've never had a doctor in the family. Another said, "By the time you have a practice, all of us here will be old enough to be regular customers." My father seemed to glow, but then he said he was going to the kitchen to see if the heart, liver, and gizzard were ready to eat. My mother was waiting for him in the kitchen doorway. They sat together in the dining room until the third quarter was nearly over.

Saturday night I went to my former high school's senior class play with a friend, something, at least, to escape watching Lawrence Welk and *Perry Mason* with my parents. On the way home, my friend had his father's car up to sixty on the narrow, two-lane that snaked past the streets where we lived half a mile apart. Less than half a mile from my street, a car backed out onto the road, and when my friend punched the brakes hard, the car four-wheel drifted to the right as I gripped the door handle and watched the world turn green with hedges that shielded a cement wall. Then the car spun, the tires caught, and we rocked to a stop parallel to that backed-out car. "He must have shit himself," my friend said. "Good thing I knew what to do." It sounded like he was excited we'd almost died. When I walked inside my house a minute later, my parents were watching the news. I didn't say anything but "I'm back."

In my room, the radio on to settle me down, I thought about how, in seventh grade, that friend who was driving hadn't been chosen to be a whiz kid, but he'd graduated with better grades than I had, just missing salutatorian. He'd always been a better driver, no doubt about that. And I thought I knew why my friend had sounded the way he had. I felt experienced. I had a secret.

I played a few minutes of garbage time in two or three December basketball games. My roommate threw up after a party that offered free beer, one that I missed because of an away game.

Christmas was no different than the ones I'd celebrated before college. Church on Christmas Eve, another dinner at my grandfather's. A quartet of uncles sang their songs of expectation in unison. My mother wore the same wig as she had at Thanksgiving. I went to a party at the home of one of the two whiz-kid girls. Nobody drank anything but Coke.

New Year's Eve, I rode to the Belmar theater in Homewood with the whiz kid shortstop in his father's Peugeot to see a triple feature of Edgar Allan Poe thrillers. That part of Pittsburgh was what my parents called "a colored neighborhood." Admission was so cheap we expected broken, empty seats, a janitor hobbling the aisle with an early broom and bag while Vincent Price let loose his laugh on the screen.

The Belmar, though, was crowded. We stumbled over sets of feet as we squeezed into a row near the front, entering in mid-feature, half an hour before the House of Usher tumbled. We settled back to watch Monsieur Valdemar melt into phantasmagoric gore. Before the credits rolled for *The Pit and the Pendulum*, the house lights went up, and we saw ourselves whiter than white. The aisle clotted, black and loud, but everyone ignored us. We worked the crowd's rhythm so perfectly into our shoes we managed to bump nobody in that swirl from behind or the side, impeding none of the three hundred black patrons who never seemed to see us. In less than a minute, we walked speechless into the cataract gray of near midnight, snow swirling around the tracks we made toward that foreign car.

Twenty minutes later, my friend's mother made us each what she called a highball. "There's no harm in having one," she said. "You should celebrate not running into trouble over that way." I said nothing about the fact that I was swallowing my first drink.

My grades arrived the following week. My mother was pleased. "He won't say so, but your father is happy, too," she said, "but he wanted to know why you had that one B of yours in your math class after being in all those special classes through high school."

"Everybody in the room was in a special class in high school," I said, though I had no idea whether that was true.

Second Semester

The first day of second semester, Terry D wasn't standing beside me in eight a.m. gym. I'd heard, as soon as I'd got back to school, that he'd been killed in a car crash the week before. Somebody whose name I didn't know was to my right. After roll was called, I reminded the wrestling coach I was excused from gym because of basketball. "That will be over in a month," he said, "then you're back here at eight sharp." I decided not to tell him I would be excused again once tennis season started, receiving another one credit of A. I had three cuts, enough time for the courts to shed winter and practice to begin. I'd be on the official roster sent to all the gym teachers by the coach.

The first weekend of the second semester, I attended my first keg party. It was love at first sight. I told myself, only on weekends, a vow I thought I could keep.

The senior chemistry lab assistant told everybody that Ranger VI had hit the moon on Groundhog Day, but it failed to send back any messages. "We need to get our act together," the lab assistant said. I'd never heard of Ranger VI. I hadn't been in the television room since Kennedy. A few days later I made my way downstairs and stood in a crowd to watch the Beatles on Ed Sullivan. The night before, after my second keg party. I'd thrown up in the bushes behind the dorm, congratulating myself on how discreet I could be.

The professor in charge of chemistry recitation had been raised and educated in the Soviet Union. Each week his tone sounded to me as if it was overstuffed with condescension, asking his questions in a way that showed he expected weak, insufficient answers. One morning, he stopped in front of where I slouched in my chair. "Sit up straight," he said in a voice that made it clear good posture was mandatory, and I did.

"What an asshole," I said to half a dozen classmates after we were dismissed, but I knew that professor controlled the class participation grade that was factored into the semester grade for chemistry. Though bad posture could be considered bad class participation, what I was angry about was how I'd acquiesced to authority.

In advanced calculus, another B in math rapidly became a fantasy. I moved from anxiety and embarrassment to shame and despair. The professor returned the first test in the order, from best to worst, of grades received. Near the end, there were only two of us left without a returned test. He seemed to relish having suspense before he handed a test to a guy seated three rows away from me. It took the professor a few seconds to make his way back to my desk with that last-place exam, a 40% that he mercifully did not announce aloud.

The failure in calculus settled in like a long hangover. French was a hassle to attend at eight a.m. Chemistry had moved past material I was previously familiar with. Arranged alphabetically by our initials, our test grades were posted beside the professor's office door. GWF's first test score was 83. Not only did I have to remind myself nearly every day to study, I struggled just to do laundry and make my bed. To rise from filthy sheets and attend a lecture, so unprepared for class participation that I kept my head down as if I was about to vomit. "You're becoming a familiar story," a girl I went out with said. While I was trying to make out whether or not she was being sympathetic, she said she'd prefer folk medicine, miracles and prayer to my future medical care.

I started leaving chemistry lab early. Three hours was exhausting. Sometimes I managed to finish an experiment if a miracle occurred in less than two. Usually I asked a chemistry major who lived just down the hall from me, "What did you get?" as if I were comparing results, as if I wasn't working backward from his answer to produce a semblance of proper procedure.

Before long, Monday, Wednesday, and Friday became the best days for waking near noon, when calculus and chemistry and French were nearly ended and the gang shower was deserted. Tuesday and Thursday were a relief. I attended history and literature, classes where I did the reading and didn't dread being a fool.

Spring break was a week stuck in Pittsburgh while the weather was still problematic. After I received an F in calculus at mid-terms, the grades arriving home before I could escape, my father asked me if I knew the story of how janitors were once hired in Alamogordo, New Mexico, whether the name of that town meant something or if I'd stopped thinking altogether about anything but my present self.

"The atomic bomb," I said, but he went on as if I hadn't answered.

"If you couldn't read a word, you were hired. They wanted illiterates to do that work in New Mexico."

We were together in a restaurant. I had been born, within a few weeks, of the atom bomb's first test. I was supposed to become a doctor, not clean up after their accomplishments, somebody who'd never know their secrets, a failure sweeping up in ignorance. I knew that he meant me to sense that all I might ever be was a patient; that all I'd be able to do was listen while the way my life would close was decided outside of my control, an illiterate in New Mexico.

"The scientists," he said, "were creating the end of the world while those janitors, unaware of their secrets, emptied trash." Lips moving, he calculated a tip before sliding three quarters and two dimes under his plate, waiting for me to stand, leaving my grades open on the table because I needed to understand that anyone, even a busboy, could recognize I was as helpless as those illiterates in New Mexico.

That night, out with two girls and a friend who followed me home in his car, I believed I was being thoughtful as I carefully opened the garage by hand to park my parents' car inside.

Because we thought it was cool to stay up until sunrise, last beers standing open for more than an hour, I was awake and dressed at five-thirty when my mother called that friend's house because she needed to be at work. "The driveway and your bed," she said, "were both empty," crying because my small kindness, so unexpected, had brought her anger, and then a near-paralysis of fear.

My mother drove off in time, and I walked outside into the same weather my mother felt at the bakery door my father unlocked for her before six each Saturday, returning to doughnuts and eclairs, the most perishable items he sold made last. Outside, the scream inside my ears dialed back to buzz, and I believed I was myself again.

We drove those girls to the houses in which they lived before it was fully light outside. One sat beside me, knees drawn up to her chin like a pouting child. Expectation is the only thing that had happened between us, the car's radio full of the British Invasion until I followed her under the driveway's double floodlights to the house I would never be inside. "Next time you're home," she said, before my friend and I pulled away and drove, a few miles later, past where she would die in another boy's new sports car the following week. It was a place I'd seen so often, I noticed nothing but oncoming headlights, ones kept on by cautious drivers even as the light improved. I switched the radio in my friend's car to Marvin Gaye and James Brown, the road so familiar I didn't worry as he became careless with the speed limit.

"You have the blahs," my mother said when I saw her later, true enough, since I was already failing one course, two more with Cs. Even then, before those cautionary grades became final, I couldn't see why my parents said nothing. Why my mother, after working from six to six, made fried chicken and corn that night as if her remission was something to be tested by exhaustion. Why my father read the newspaper while he ate, his plate turning white with coagulated grease beneath bones. Why she washed dishes while I showered and dressed before borrowing the car again as they settled in to watch Lawrence Welk. But mostly why I thought melancholy was a way of life or preparing me for discovery.

When I used my first away tennis match as an excuse for taking a test late and the professor gave me the same test that a friend provided to sample problems he had solved, I managed only a 55. All that was left was the chance I might get above a 70 on the final.

One morning, the present felt crumpled like scratch paper after an exam. That wadded ball unfolded wrinkled and smaller and whimpering until I smothered it in my fist. All day I was leery of numbers that chattered like reunion relatives: square roots and functions, molecular weights of compounds. Already the slide rule was a set of footprints that ended in a steep drop into water. The day I gave up medicine, Lyndon Johnson declared a war on poverty, but I didn't learn that until the semester ended because I didn't read a newspaper or hadn't watched television since that night with the Beatles.

Later that day, a girl I wanted to have sex with said I should be tested for the name of my problems, sounding like a family doctor handing me off to an expensive specialist. I slipped my hand under her blouse, thinking nothing about the medical terms for arousal, intent upon the anatomy of desire. Whatever she felt for the next few minutes, our separation had already begun.

Easter came early in 1964, Good Friday on the 27th of March. As always, my father closed the bakery from noon to three, and I, home again, was expected to sit through all seven words of the Cross. Nearly every churchgoer came and went between the words, spending anywhere from twenty minutes to an hour. Except for me and my parents. We lasted through "I thirst," "Why have you forsaken me," and "It is finished" as if Good Friday service was the equivalent of chemistry lab. We sang the doleful hymns. The minister worked seven variations on sacrifice and martyrdom before he released us to blink in the late March sun. My mother, at three p.m., reopened the bakery for workers whose shifts were never adjusted for God. My father slept and ate and drove me back to sugar, salt, flour and grease by seven because my mid-term failure made me feel obligated to pitch in and help until midnight for some sort of atonement.

We were side by side at 9:26 EST in Etna, Pennsylvania, the work room filled with the smell of yeast. My father, because it was still Good Friday, refused the red radio until midnight, instead humming the old hymns, keeping the last hours holy, when an extraordinary earthquake struck Alaska. Though neither of us knew anything about it until five minutes of news came on the radio at midnight just as he turned it on as a signal I was excused.

The next night, as I was leaving the house, I told my parents that I'd changed my major to English. I came home late enough to be certain they were asleep.

My father didn't talk to me at breakfast and on the way to church. My mother passed my news along to a couple of aunts after the service. She took me aside to confirm what I already knew. "Your father is disappointed," she said. "He doesn't know what he's paying for now."

At my grandfather's, while we ate ham and scalloped potatoes, one uncle said, "I hear you're an English major now. What's that all about—pre-law?"

My father looked stricken. "Maybe," I started in, then decided against lying and added, "probably not."

An aunt said, "I know. You want to be a teacher."

"No," I said at once, sure of myself on that guess.

A moment passed. "What else is there?" my uncle said.

"That's what I'll find out, I guess," I said.

My uncle looked at my father. "Sounds like you're paying for a mighty expensive scavenger hunt." I knew what my father was thinking: English is fuzzy and feminine, an easy major that means his son is an academic coward.

Once basketball had ended, I had begun drinking a few weekday evenings a week in a townie bar that served underage. Like nearly everyone, I ordered Iron City drafts that came in ten-ounce glasses for fifteen cents each. Alone sometimes, head down, I listened to men my father's age complain about politics and work.

I was always waiting for a story to tell, and one night, before I finished three beers, it came in the shape of a man who stumbled down the backroom's flight of stairs holding a knife anybody could tell he'd been stabbed with. Ashen and sweating, he mumbled his way to a booth and performed the dead-man's drop. Like me, the men seated nearby watched him in the mirror above a sculpture of bottles while the bartender dialed the phone beside the cash register.

For three minutes, no one ordered or spoke. Siren wailing, an ambulance arrived seconds after two bellied policemen. As if he'd been summoned, a shirtless man came down the stairs to surrender. "Stop me," one cop said, "if you've heard this one before," and from both sides of me stories started about an earlier upstairs stabbing, one from the year before.

Weeks went by, nothing worth retelling except the night that stabbing victim, apparently recovered, sat at the bar and nobody asked him about anything but high school football and basketball.

His assailant sat beside him, and I felt older knowing men returned to habits as easily as swallowing beer, that they could even fall asleep in the same room while jukebox rock and roll rose through the floor, and I sat infatuated with small experiments in self-destruction.

All that protected me was silence and quarters I slotted one after the other like a townie who wanted to be liked by playing Fifties music, somebody whose father surely worked with steel or coal.

At the spring honors convocation in mid-April, I was announced as the male recipient of the freshman scholarship. The award was for the combination of first semester grade point and a multiple-choice test that reminded me of the verbal SAT, the test that the school had used to place me in advanced composition.

The donor wanted to meet me and the female recipient. I recognized her. She was the only other freshman who had been placed in advanced composition first semester. I'd never spoken to her. My calculus professor walked past in his academic regalia and seemed to squint when he saw me.

In May, in a low-budget Cleveland hotel, I watched my doubles partner snap the arms off both chairs in the room another doubles team from our college was sharing. Drunk, he'd decided he wanted them to witness a show of force, sitting to flex his arms to the side. Hiroshima, he said, triumphant, and as if they needed to understand, he reseated himself for Nagasaki, laughing and leaving them to wonder. For two days, he had been my ally in a college conference tournament we hadn't won. The following week, I'd receive my first F and learn, when I moved back in with my parents for the summer, that my father would continue his Easter break refusal to speak.

My second day at home, borrowing the car while my father slept after his night shift at the bakery, I noticed a neighbor at the bus stop at the end of our street. He was older than my father, but now he looked ancient, stooped and fragile, and I offered him a ride. He sat beside me and said he was going grocery shopping at the Giant Eagle along the highway a couple of miles away, that he didn't drive anymore, launching into his colostomy story, his liver cancer sequel, ending with "I'm still here today" and "I'm buying food." He smiled as I dropped him off at the grocery. "Maybe you'll be the one discovers a cure for this mess," he said.

I didn't tell him I was no longer pre-med. I said, "Sure thing," driving off to a factory job interview daydreaming about my F of calculus, his F of tumors, and what seemed to be the passing grade my mother had received, all of them assigned by the hit and miss of luck. Though I thought, finally, that all of my ambition had suffered a form of congestive failure.

"Go to work," my mother said at ten o'clock. "It's his last night. Surprise him." Her hair had returned. She'd given those wigs back to my aunt. She knew that my father wasn't about to tell me that he had decided to close the bakery. "He got himself a job as janitor at the high school," she said. "He says it's because it's too hard to make ends meet, but I know it's because of what's been going on with me this last year."

My father nodded when I walked in. He turned the radio on. In Etna, that last night of baking, he marked the early hours with the same scheduled hand-work as always—bread and sandwich buns being readied or already baking. When my father spoke to me for the first time since March, I knew my mother had been working on him since Easter. He told me to go home and sleep, and then, as if it was an afterthought, he said he needed me the next afternoon, so be around.

The next afternoon, in the day's full heat, there was one wedding cake, three tiers, the bride and groom standing in a white gazebo that needed to fit inside a circle of sugar roses and loops of icing. My father ordered me to drive so he could balance that beauty nine miles, three of them to avoid the cobblestones of a neighborhood called Cabbage Hill to the Cherry City Fire Hall where women were preparing golabkies, pierogies, and kielbasa, sweating in a windowless small kitchen.

He retouched those swirls of icing and laid that white gazebo just right, erasing the dot of icing that reminded him which part of those circles faced front. Those women praised the cake and offered beer, Iron City on tap, but my father waved his spatula until one of them fished out a bottle of cherry soda from a cooler packed with ice. She looked at me, and I nodded, accepting the same, able to wait three hours to drink myself stupid with a girl I planned to never marry, allowing my father to take his time with the end of baking, standing beside the cake until he decided to drive back to the bakery where my mother, near closing, would be offering everything for half price.

"I could have kept this going," he said as soon as we were in the car. "You understand what I mean by that?"

I nodded. And I did. It would kill my mother, maybe, and because hiring a full-time salesperson would erase the thin margin of profit. Because, feeling useless, my mother would refuse to quit until she dropped or her still-unspoken "health problems" returned. Or what would never be said, because it would take his legs out from under him or cloud his lungs and, unlike the janitor position, there was no safety net of social security or medical insurance or retirement plan and never had been.

"Get up for church tomorrow," he said then. He didn't say anything else, but that one extra sentence felt like acknowledgement by indirection, that beginning the next day he'd return to a few comments about sports and church, leaving unspoken that janitor was a job that suggested failure as much as the English major did, that we both had something to prove. He wasn't self-sufficient, my mother was mortal, and "whiz-kid" was a name more appropriate for those who hadn't yet been tested.

Sunday night I drove to a high school graduation party for a girl I'd been out with a few times. After it ended, as I approached the railroad tracks that crossed the highway a block from my father's bakery, the red lights began flashing and the crossing gates lowered. I could see there was no train coming up from the south. Impatient, I slowed and glanced up the tracks to the north, noticing the train seemed far enough away to beat. "Here we go," I said, like I'd done it before, pulling around the gate and bouncing over two sets of tracks, the train, running downhill, something I hadn't fully considered, flashing behind us a second later.

That girl caught her breath as if she were resurfacing from a minute underwater. Neither of us spoke, not even when she left the car and hurried up the driveway to her house without waiting for me to walk beside her. I idled at the curb like a taxi driver who believed he was protecting the vulnerable from possible harm. She never looked back.

A Short History of Hair

Near the end of May, 1965, with just a week of final exams left in my sophomore year of college, I spent a Saturday afternoon bleaching my hair.

I had help, my roommate and another fraternity brother who claimed he knew just how much hydrogen peroxide would make us blond. After a few beers, I believed him.

My brown hair had grown past my collar, a length that drew suspicion even on campus. My roommate's light brown hair was clipped short; the other guy still slicked his black hair back like Elvis.

The three of us soaked our hair and, satisfied we were about to be transformed, we went outside to lie in the sun, drink more beer, and wait for blondness to arrive. We checked every half hour, looking in gang bathroom's mirrors. In between visits, we evaluated the color of the hair we could see and shared assessments. By the end of the afternoon, my roommate was solidly blond. I was blond with streaks of orange. The other guy's hair turned an unsettling, alien shade of orange.

I took my finals as a blond and spent the first afternoon at home at a picnic with my parents and the family of one of my mother's brothers, who had promised me, during spring break, that he would get me a summer job at Heinz.

He was white-collar, a manager and, according to my mother, "a bigwig." Before I'd finished my first hamburger, he told me, "You have to get a haircut or I can't speak for you."

His older daughter chimed in. "I think it's cute. He looks like one of the Beach Boys. Like a surfer."

My uncle frowned. "We don't need surfers at Heinz."

The next afternoon I cut the grass, my father welcoming me home for that particular job. My blond hair stuck to my neck and shoulders. I was shirtless, sweat forming quickly. Our neighbor Mr. Ratliff nodded my way as he stood smoking on his back porch. It wasn't a friendly nod. It was the sort of nod that might ID a criminal in a lineup. He was a union man, a teamster. His son, a year younger than me, was in Vietnam, volunteering for the Navy fresh out of high school.

My mother was waiting in the kitchen when I came inside. "Your father will be happy you went straight out and took care of the grass," she said.

"I've been doing it for years," I said, but she placed a hand on my arm as if she needed my attention. "Your father won't say it, but he's worried that you'll let your hair make you miss your chance."

"Chance at what?"

"Real work," she said, drawing her hand away. "Being useful."

"Somebody he can be proud of," I said, letting bitterness seep into my voice.

"Yes," she said, but she looked stricken, her lips pressing together as if she'd revealed too much of a long-held secret. She opened her left hand, the one that she'd kept at her side, and showed me a five-dollar bill. "If there's change," she said, "you can keep it. Just do what needs to be done."

I took that tiny bribe and knew she'd call her brother before I got home. All I had to do was endure the barber's jokes. He'd cut my hair since elementary school, half of those years just trimming down my flat top and selling me occasional tubes of gunk that kept it stiff. "I'll bet your old man told you to get in this chair pronto," he said right off, but what he settled on discussing was the shade of my hair.

"You do a bleach job on yourself?" he said, and when I nodded, he added, "You looking to stay blond? You want a real dye job?"

A man my father's age reading a *Life* magazine laughed, which seemed to inspire the barber. "Bleaching your hair like that makes you go bald faster," he said. "I'll bet you that makes you think twice about keeping yourself blond." More laughter from behind the *Life*. A few minutes later, I used the change to buy two slices of pepperoni and anchovy pizza.

By the time I arrived home and washed the grease from my hands, my mother told me I had an interview at nine a.m. sharp two days from then.

By 9:15 I'd filled out an application and handed it to a secretary, who passed it along to a man in a suit and tie. I was wearing a similar outfit, sport coat and tie, but when he called me into his office, the interview seemed so routine that when he reached the phrase "We'll contact you if anything opens up," I felt like Samson wishing for my hair back.

I waited to hear if there was anything else that might signal opportunity, and then, just as I resigned myself to standing, my uncle appeared. "Glen," he said, extending his hand, "I see you've already met my nephew."

This time, when I reached home, my mother told me that Heinz had called. I was to report for work Monday morning at 7:45. I needed to be there at 7:30 so I could get my uniform and punch in before 7:45. The rest I'd find out. "See?" she said. "See how just a little bit of compromise goes a long way?"

Sunday night, I went to a series of high school graduation parties with RuthAnn McIntyre, a girl I'd been going out with during breaks from college. My mother dropped me off at the apartment where the first party was happening. "Why does she have to be Catholic?" was her only anxiety. "We sent you to a Lutheran college." I had to find my own ride home.

RuthAnn said she loved my blond hair, but why was it so streaked? "I didn't know what I was doing" was my quick explanation. "I probably didn't soak my head evenly or something."

"You know what I heard about how the Romans used to do that way back when?"

"No idea," I said. I wanted to get my hands on one of the bottles of beer soaking in a tub of ice.

"Pigeon poop."

"Who told you that?"

"I go to an all-girls' school," she said. "Hair is a big deal." And then she forgot about my hair, and we settled into having a few beers before somebody gave us a ride to a house with a large, finished basement that featured an enormous stereo. The first thing I heard there besides The

Supremes was some high school kid observing that the only people he knew who bleached their hair were girls and queers.

It was just after three a.m. when that same boy dropped me off, but not before he spent seven miles of the eight-mile trip bragging about how well he could drive drunk. I didn't argue his sociology or his driving skill. By that hour of the morning, my mother's 6:15 wake-up call was as threatening as a funnel cloud.

At 6:30, as promised, she served me eggs I could barely finish. I nibbled at toast to settle my stomach and grimaced at the orange juice. She drove me into Pittsburgh and dropped me off at the entrance at 7:25. "You're on your own now," she said. "All grown up."

The equipment man had my name. He handed me a pair of pin-striped blue and white pants, a couple of white t-shirts and several paper hats. I punched in at 7:43 and found my way to where unlabeled institution-sized cans were entering a room on three conveyor belts, each of them with a man clearing them onto metal trays that were eight-deep and raised to be filled, one by one, by lever. The work was simple. All it took was the ability not to be distracted by dreams of the day ending.

A half hour in, as if someone had just realized I needed to pass a physical before something happened and the company was liable, I was hustled to the medical center. A nurse ran me through a cursory exam. She told me I needed a tuberculosis test and punctured my upper left arm. Nothing to it, except when I stood, I fainted and fell onto her, dragging her to the floor. Her screams quickly snapped me back. I crawled off as the doctor appeared.

"You stay out late last night and barely eat this morning?" he asked. When I nodded, he began to regale me with stories of his own college days full of hangovers. I was happy to sit through them. He was more entertaining than a line of identical, unlabeled cans.

4:30 arrived. I was cursed in chorus at the time clock because I didn't have my card ready when I reached the front of the line. I stored that prompt for the next sixty days of exits.

I had to ride the bus home. Our family had one car, and now we had three members working. I could handle a few bus rides, couldn't I?

When I got on, I heard "Hi, Gary" from a mid-bus seat. "What are you doing on here?" Roseanne Ratliff said. She was a year older than me and a lot friendlier than her father. A secretary now. Used to riding back and forth. "My dad said you looked like something the cat dragged in. I guess you got a haircut since he saw you."

"I had to. The job," I said.

"But you're so blond. That's cool. And anyway, my dad is probably jealous, him and his chrome dome since I can remember. I bet my little brother doesn't stand a chance."

"He didn't look jealous. He looked like he wanted to come over and slap me."

Roseanne smiled. "You want to know a secret?" she said. "My dad said you didn't look like anybody who was worth a good goddamn."

I managed a week with the cans, keeping up with the line in a way that got the foreman to relax. I traded in my pants and shirts on Friday and got a new supply. On Saturday, I went out shirtless to cut grass again and right away noticed several cars parked along the street in front of our neighbor's house. Roseanne was nowhere to be seen. More cars arrived before I finished.

Inside, my mother stopped me before I unplugged the radio to carry outside. "Tommy Ratliff has been killed," my mother said. "The word has been getting around all morning."

Instead of lying out in the sun with the radio, I took a shower. Tommy had joined the Navy, seemingly out of danger. I didn't know anybody who'd been killed in Vietnam. I could barely find it on a map. The casualty counts were like the numbers for exotic faraway diseases like elephantiasis or yaws. A few dozen per week, sometimes less. It occurred to me that Tommy Ratliff might have been the only Navy casualty in the entire month of June.

It seemed more dangerous to ride in cars with my friends. Speed was mandatory. Drinking was too. Nobody wore a seat belt. And always, there was AM rock radio at maximum volume. The weekend before, I'd screamed along with a friend to Wooly Bully and Satisfaction, absorbing every perfect note. I was still blond, hoping to turn some female heads.

I turned on the news and listened to a report on the battle of Dong Xoai—the number of dead Americans was tentative, but it seemed as if nineteen US soldiers had been killed there in the past four days. Hundreds of VietCong were announced dead. Wasn't that a major victory? Somehow it didn't sound that way, and now General Westmoreland was asking for a big run up of additional troops.

I went out with RuthAnn. We played mini-golf, a game I'd loved ten years earlier. We watched a movie on her parents' television and didn't touch each other until she followed me to the car I could borrow on a Saturday night because no one in my family worked then. "You don't have to worry," she said. "You're in college. Two years from now this will all be over."

She was right, I thought. The Cold War was the big deal. The space race. The United States had Gemini 4 in space orbiting over and over. One of the astronauts had even gone outside the ship.

Meanwhile, the Soviet Union had aimed a rocket at the moon—Luna 6—and everybody had acted as if we'd suffered another science defeat until it missed the moon by 99,000 miles and became a joke.

On Monday, I would be working in another department—sterilizing. The shift was 3:15 to midnight. Somebody would have to pick me up at 12:15 because the bus didn't run that late.

I'd walked through the sterilizing room on my way to lunch one day the week before. Huge pressure cookers, row upon row of cans shelved and installed in rounded boxcars that ran along tracks and were guided into the sterilizers by three or four men at a time because of the weight. "Sterilizing?" my uncle said. "You'll find out what work is, that's for sure."

I came home sober. I was ready on time for church the following morning.

Afterward, still wearing a sport coat and tie, I walked to our mailbox to retrieve the Sunday paper. I hoped Mr. Ratliff saw my hair was cut, that Roseanne had told him I was doing full-time blue-collar work and, after thirty days, I'd be a dues-paying member of the Amalgamated Meat Cutters and Butcher Workmen of America. A union man. Worth a good goddamn.

A Birth Primer

The Spiritualists

The year my wife and I were about to stop birth control and "let things happen," I watched a television documentary about recent incidents of premature birth that featured an astonishment of medical marvels tempered by the inclusion of problems that often follow—crippling side effects, babies precarious with pneumonia, and even one acknowledgement, despite progress, of death. I recognized the symptoms at once. A college friend and his wife, only a few weeks earlier, had suffered through a similar scenario, one that friend had memorialized with a series of slides taken hours apart during the two days his son had lived, leaving the last of those pictures on the screen until he completed his recollections while I stared at the lost, cyanotic child.

The Dark Car

One late evening, a few months later, as I began to enter freeway traffic from a narrow side street, my wife, using a tone set exactly upon obey, said "Stop" just before a car without headlights flashed by so close to us it trembled our tiny, economical German car.

We caught up to the dark car, still without headlights, as it sat at the first stoplight in one of many industrial towns along the Ohio River. A woman, we could tell, was driving. She was alone, turned left, and for a block we followed until she turned again, still dark, leaving us to cross a bridge to a second factory town before entering, with caution, the highway to our home.

By now it was late January, my wife early in pregnancy that seemed to have happened from our first unprotected sex. We'd laughed that we were like those teenage couples in the cautionary sex-ed high school films we'd once been forced to watch. But that night, when we speculated, when several miles of silence was about to end at our apartment, what I wondered was the nature of my wife's voice that made me not question her warning. Not volume, not a pitch up to panic, just precise connotation among a thousand variations of command.

Lesson One: The Evolution of Eyes

Some things we began to notice: In the discount store, the oversized eyes of babies on velvet; in the mall, a woman who drew infants with chalk; in the newspaper, a report on the craze for Big Eyes paintings; in a magazine, a discussion of the cartoon evolution of Mickey Mouse, who had rounded from rodent to child's toy, his face adorable now that it featured the sentimental safeguard of the newborn, the sugared look shared by puppies and kittens and lambs.

Maternity Ward, Visiting Hours

The last summer I had lived at home, after I sometimes borrowed my sister's car, I was responsible for picking her up where she worked as a nurse in obstetrics at a hospital named for the patron saint for a sprawling spectrum of the down and out—the falsely accused, the homeless, the orphaned, the mentally ill, and every penitent, single mother. Sometimes, when I was early, I would wait near the window where men and women stood to search incubators as if shopping for reassurance while folklore and superstition followed every doctor down the halls like spies. My sister, when I mentioned she'd chosen the best area of medicine, said, "Not always, and when it's not, it's the worst."

Commandments

Years before, my mother had told the story about a friend who had one kidney, two babies, and a doctor who said, with the next one, she would murder herself or lapse into dependency upon dialysis to drag her up from toxicity's depth. And yet, my mother had said, that woman sat there pregnant again because her church had said you can't slip anything between yourself and the next soul waiting in line to enter its earthly body.

That friend had heard the same marriage instructions my wife and I had; she'd absorbed the commandments for married life from a designated priest. And maybe someone had stood and said, "Bless us, Father," like the man next to me at our last session, minutes before we could leave and try to forget our four hours over hell. Everyone stood. We received a blessing that inferred a curse on me, starting with soiling myself and soiling others, including the woman beside me who was going to curse herself with coils and pills to keep some souls in limbo jostling for a while.

For nearly three months we stayed secretive with our news, adhering to our own superstitions about premature public exuberance. Already we had abandoned one doctor who decorated his office with posters of Bible passages with praying hands and promised to choose our child rather than my wife if an emergency arose. My sister, by now, had an advanced degree in nursing. The teaching position she had taken was at a Catholic university.

Lesson Two: The History of Lactaria

Lactaria means places of milk, the Roman columns, once, where babies were brought by mothers, sometimes for the milk of a wet nurse, though more often, perhaps, to be abandoned, the mothers trusting pity's power to save their children, what was offered by a local church after a newborn, discovered in a park, had not, despite the sweet kitsch of infancy, survived one night's exposure to a late March freeze.

What Charmed Us

In Turkey, mothers, right after giving birth, drink lohusa serbeti ("postpartum sherbet") made with water, sugar, cloves, cinnamon and red food coloring.

In Latin America, new mothers observe *la cuarentena* ("quarantine"), forty days of recuperating by abstaining from sex, physical activity and spicy foods.

What We Disagreed On

Male names
Female names

My Sister Explains her Research

Anencephalic, she said, during the last days before we announced, naming the subject of her study of ethics. I listened and said nothing and kept my expression set at neutral because she spoke as if reading from the report she'd submitted for government funding. I could see her Roman numerals and their subject headings within the cloud of her early April breath, but what I wanted to know was how an expectant mother felt, knowing the child she was carrying could not possibly survive, yet could be kept alive for hours or days in order to be harvested of its organs as long as that mother consented to carry it to term, a personal charity for the otherwise doomed. How she could accept the smiles of strangers as she swelled, the congratulations of relatives and friends unless she chose to terminate or tell she was transporting a set of parts for the needy.

What We Disagreed On

Whether I researched too much like my sister, discovering ways that made normal seem unusual.

The Stone Child

In a book about anomalies, I discovered the stone child, who remained curled twenty-eight years unborn within its mother's belly. How it was lifted into the light when she died because neighbors feared she had been taken by Satan's lust. How a Sixteenth Century autopsy found her split uterus unknowable as bacteria, that woman hauling the dead for decades like a small, untranslatable headstone.

What Charmed Us

In Germany, names that are objects (like Apple or Tree) or surnames are never allowed, and the baby's gender must be revealed by his or her first name.

In Japan, new mothers rest in bed for twenty-one days to recuperate and bond with the baby, while family members of every age do all the household chores.

After We Announced: What My Sister Stopped Saying She Had Witnessed

Down syndrome
Cerebral palsy
Cleft palate
Spina bifada
Clubfoot
Defects of the eyes and heart

After We Announced: What My Mother Gave Me

A stack of folded, white-going-to-gray cloth.

What My Mother Said

"Diapers. You'll be glad I saved them. They'll come in handy. You don't want to be buying new over and over, and don't you worry about them holding up after all these years. They worked just fine on you once upon a time."

The Dark Car 2

Because the side road we were traveling the night of our near catastrophe led to and from the campus where I was in my second year as an English instructor, I pulled out onto that freeway nearly every day. Except for the occasional trips for evening events, all of those entrances were made in daylight, but for weeks I looked to my left a second time and sometimes a third, imagining I missed the approach of a speeding car.

Every time cars shot by, I regretted not thinking to memorize a license plate or even the make and model of that nearly invisible car. Like a small child, all I could remember was that the car was dark and going fast. When I mentioned this to my wife, she said, "We have better things to do than dwell on that. It's over. We were lucky. Move on." By now, my friend's wife was pregnant again. She told us the news as soon as she knew for sure.

LaMaze

My wife bought a book and began to read. She asked me to read it, too.

Let labor begin on its own

Walk, move around and change positions throughout labor

Bring a loved one, friend or doula for continuous support

Avoid interventions that are not medically necessary

Avoid giving birth on your back and follow your body's urges to push

What Charmed Us

In the Dominican Republic, a spoon, knife and fork are placed under three different chairs, and the mother-to-be chooses one to sit on. The spoon means girl, the knife boy, the fork undetermined.

In Bali, the baby's feet can't touch the ground for 210 days. Because they are divine and sent from heaven, because the days have been measured until they can cross over to this earthly realm.

What Failed to Charm Us

Women feared for the features of their soon-to-be-born because, they'd too often seen sheep or snakes, or worse, carelessly touched them. Change, they believed, could enter children through fingers and eyes. Sometimes, infants slid into breath with the facial hair of wolves or the snouts of pigs, midwives cursing the quirks of God, and once, a woman woke to a monkey perched so high on her inner thigh, she birthed the world's tiniest child, renaming her The Sicilian Fairy and displaying that girl until, at nine years old, she died.

What My Wife Did

My wife didn't smoke and gave up alcohol. She moved dangerous household products to high shelves and padded the corners of furniture.

What My Wife Said

"Proactive is for the commonplace. Anxiety is for the rare."

The Stone Child 2

Early that summer, a woman who worked with my wife told her that someone she knew had learned that the child she carried would die shortly after birth. A doctor had listed the critical missing pieces in her unborn's body as if, our small suburb mostly bare of animals, absence was the thing capable of harm. Although surprise was obsolete, she had chosen to carry hopelessness to term, her beliefs gathered to dust for the faint fingerprints of choice, that brief, good thing, her son's impossible cry sung through her, pitched so high it sounded like breathing.

What Charmed Us

In Nigeria, babies are given water (to have no enemies), palm oil (for a smooth, stress-free life), kola nut (for a long and healthy one), and salt and pepper (to keep things exciting and spicy).

In Pennsylvania, in that year before sonograms were commonplace, one doctor predicted a girl, born late, while one, laughing, said his colleague had graduated from the school of old wives' tales.

Lesson Three: What's been Asked of Wives

In the South American cultures where a multiple birth means the woman has cheated on her husband, what's needed is a private, discreet disposal to save a marriage.

What's good is getting to a private place before they're born, letting each of them slide secretly into their birthdays, giving the chosen some comfort like heaven's guide.

What's best is "the death without pain at all," pressing their chests before they draw a breath. Keep them from cold and claws. Use kindnesses so instinctive they rush to help like faith.

Above all, do not dwell on their faces. As much as possible, do not touch them.

Go home with the baby you fiercely love. If all goes well, you will be forgiven.

LaMaze 2

In a room set aside in a neighboring town's community center, my wife and I attended a demonstration class. Six couples followed a woman's directions about how to control pain through a loved one's support and the mother-to-be's practiced panting each time the pain of a contraction reoccurred.

Lesson Four: Why SIDS is More Likely

From sleeping on the stomach or side.

From sleeping on a soft surface.

From lying face down on a fluffy comforter, a soft mattress or a waterbed.

From sharing a bed with parents, siblings, or pets.

From being too warm while sleeping.

From being premature.

Revisiting the Legends

In the stories retold for centuries, a child is raised by wolves; others are nurtured by baboons or a miscellany of friendly forest creatures. Yet once, at the college my wife and I had attended, a student, without the subsidy of folklore or religion, gave birth in the privacy of her spring break dorm room, then wrapped and disposed of that child inside a week's worth of clean sheets and towels. For years, the story was passed down to every dorm resident. After decades passed, it became something like a legend.

LaMaze 3

Sometimes, in the car, when a radio song began, I would choke my wife's thigh just above her knee, and she would startle, then pant until I relaxed, watching the highway with one hand on the wheel, gripping her again near the end of the radio's song, that interval a sign of urgency, that contraction insistent with imminence, and she would close her eyes for the darkness of realism, riding tensed and blind in the passenger seat, poised for the claw that demanded her practiced, rapid breathing.

What We Disagreed On

Whether she should be driving when I clutched her thigh.
Whether my refusal meant I was cautious or controlling.

The Impossible

A local woman gave birth in her bathtub, then allowed her newborn daughter to drown. She told her boyfriend to carry the baby outside and stuff it deep and fully covered in their garbage can, "Now I lay me down to sleep," the boyfriend testified he had prayed over the baby's body when he had wrapped it in plastic and buried it under leaves rather than plunging it in garbage. To show his concern for the child, he said. To show he wasn't heartless, not like his girlfriend who'd also stuffed toilet paper down the baby's throat. "Blue," he said. "The toilet paper was light blue," as if he needed, just then, to colorize death.

The Possible

"None of those stories have anything to do with us," my wife said. "Worry about the possible if you have to worry." My wife's mother, when she visited, lapsed into the story of a relative who had brought home her healthy baby, nursed it nine days, and then dropped it. "Nine days," she said, like it was the title of a book we should read. "The baby died."

Runway

When a gate across the airport service road was left open, we entered like extras early in disaster movies, the couple who carelessly confront the overloaded, late-rising cargo plane, and I paused on the upslope, cautious and choosing blindly where a runway ended just above, planes taking off at seven-minute intervals like early contractions, both of us holding our breath after we'd timed a takeoff past six, expectant, proximity to size and power calling up a mix of thrill and terror. "Let's go," my wife said after the third plane. "This is awful." I kept us there for five.

The Day After Planes

Morning:

My wife keeps her scheduled doctor's appointment. The younger doctor at the office predicts a girl and late, relying on the way she is carrying the fetus. He tells her he is opposed to my being in the delivery room. "There's a reason it's never happened before in our hospital. Things can go wrong, and if he can't handle it, he's a problem nobody needs."

Afternoon:

My wife says she is having contractions. "They're pretty far apart," she says. "It's probably false labor. The doctor just said the baby will be late. Go play tennis like you planned. I'll just relax and then start dinner in an hour or so."

Early evening:

I leave the courts early. The contractions, when I get home, have become more intense. They arrive more frequently. Dinner is postponed. "It's going to be a month early," my wife says. "It's like those airplanes started something."

Late evening:

The practice's older doctor is on call. He welcomes my intention to be in the delivery room and predicts nothing except the expectation of a successful birth. "This is late-term premature," he says. "The best kind." I tell him about his colleague's prediction. "Dr. Nostradamus," he says and laughs. "He gets his share of coin flips." In the delivery room, my wife pants. The nurses inspect and then ignore me. When the doctor says, "You have time to get something to eat," I follow him out.

Midnight:

"I know where you ate dinner," my wife says. "Chili dogs with onions are unmistakable." Then she pants.

Lesson Five: Early Morning

First, notice the doctor's car radio glowing below the hospital window, the lot, after midnight, nearly empty, announcing there is time, yet, to listen for a baseball game's outcome formed by extra innings.

Second, wait in a dressing room as if you have an appointment.

At last, pay attention when the doctor returns and offers scrubs, saying, "The Pirates won, put these on." Now slowly dress, becoming who you have asked to be, the first father permitted in that hospital's delivery room.

Feel how the nurses, one young and one old, wish you were elsewhere while you encourage and your wife pants. Suspect that the doctor is sparing you by never once mentioning problems made more likely by early delivery.

Listen to the nurses' voices say "push," sounding like old friends. Hear blessing in the doctor's matter-of-fact assurance even as the nurses shift to a unison "boy" just before everybody's speech is paused by the first long expletive of presence, despite, regardless, and notwithstanding.

Buffalo

Scofflaw

I was sixteen the first time I was in a police station. My mother took me inside after I received my first traffic ticket.

My violation was making a U-turn around a median strip at the end of the block where my father's bakery was located. I'd made that turn every early Saturday morning after I finished my overnight shift at the bakery, working until around 5:30 a.m. before driving the station wagon home so my mother could drive to the bakery to open the store at six a.m.

But that Friday night, because I was scheduled to take the SATs Saturday morning, I'd worked from seven to eleven the way I had from eighth to tenth grade. My mother had made that U-turn every time she'd picked me up at eleven, and so did I, completing it, that night, while a police car sat at the light.

"Whose name is on that ticket?" my mother said when I showed it to her. She was in her pajamas, but she buttoned a coat up over them and slipped on a pair of shoes while I tried to make out the signature.

"Ralph something," I said.

"Ralphie Stumpf," she muttered, grabbing her keys. "You bring that thing with you, and we'll see about this."

"Is Ralph Stumpf here?" my mother asked the policeman at the desk as soon as we were inside the station.

"No, Ruthie," the policeman said, and I quietly marveled.

"Ralphie Stumpf," my mother said. "I've known him since he was in diapers."

"I expect so, Ruthie." The policeman suddenly sighed and looked old enough to retire on the spot.

My mother showed him the ticket. "Everybody makes this turn," she said. "I can name people you wouldn't dare ticket who make that turn. You know who I'm talking about. Prominent people who have businesses on that block."

"You don't know that for a fact, Ruthie," the policeman said, but he allowed us to sit down to wait.

A few minutes later, I recognized the policeman who'd written my ticket as he walked through an inside door. My mother tugged me to my feet as she rose from her chair. "Ralphie Stumpf," she waded in, repeating her assertion about the prominent people who disregarded the law. The policeman looked more embarrassed than angry, and I drifted a few steps away from the conversation, hoping that Ralph Stumpf didn't begin interrogating me. I wanted my mother to stop. I wanted to pay the ticket and get out of there.

A minute later, Ralph Stumpf tore up the ticket and my mother walked out of the station in triumph "You see?" she said. "You have to know how to deal with these people," she said. "I hope you learned something."

Fourteen years later, I tried to remember just what it was I'd learned that late evening when, after lunch near the end of June, I received a call from Sam Stambaugh, who identified himself as the county constable and said he'd been chasing after me for a couple of months. "Since April. Almost three months now, and no luck at all until today. You don't reside where your registration says you do."

"What registration?" I asked.

Stambaugh didn't seem to hear me. "I went to your apartment on 19th Street," he went on, "and the people I talked to said you didn't live there anymore."

"I moved."

"Your registration says you didn't. I checked it through Harrisburg three times. You don't just take somebody's word on this. You don't do this job for long and still believe every neighbor you come across. Finding you has cost me an awful lot of time."

"I'm in the phone book," I tried, but I started considering whether constable was a patronage job, whether Sam Stambaugh was an idiot but had a brother or an uncle in the right place to hand him something to do.

"Harrisburg finally nailed your address for me. I have a warrant here with your name on it, and I can drive out there and serve it, but I thought I'd do you a favor and call to see if you'd come in on your own.

I found out you teach at the college, so I figured you for somebody reasonable. You're a doctor, so I can call instead of driving out."

His tone made me decide to be diplomatic. "I appreciate that, " I said, "but what's the problem?"

"Scofflaw. A fine outstanding for too long."

Now I felt lost, like maybe there was someone else with the same name who lived in Beaver County. A long shot, but possible. "What fine?"

"It's just scofflaw. A couple of minutes at the JPs."

"Somebody's made a mistake."

"Couple of minutes, OK?," Stambaugh said, sounding as old and tired as that long ago cop who immediately recognized my mother. "Help us both out."

It seemed easy to comply, but I wondered what Stambaugh, the respecter of advanced degrees and college instructors, would think if he found out I would be officially out of work in less than a week. Maybe he would show up with lights flashing and sirens wailing.

I didn't have his enthusiasm for the two-year college where I would be employed for only a few more days. After five years of teaching the same two composition courses and having to stick to reading lists and assignments prescribed on a syllabus created by the main campus faculty, I'd become impatient. The year before, I'd received a PhD in Modern American Literature, and during the intervening months I'd published scholarship, how-to articles about teaching, and poems in magazines with circulations from tens of thousands to merely tens. Nobody else in the English department had published a word since I'd been hired, and six months earlier, I'd suggested to the Director of Adjunct Campuses who visited once a year from the far away main campus that maybe there were alternatives to being told how to teach, what to teach, and when to teach it. He had looked at me and suggested I should begin to search for another job if I felt that way.

"Ok," I said. "I'll do that," not exactly what he wanted to hear. To make things worse, I had made it clear to the on-campus administrator to whom I reported that I had to "de-prepare" to teach my classes in order to meet the requirements I was expected to abide by. Two months later I was out of a job.

When I arrived at the Magistrate's office, it looked empty except for a secretary who seemed to be expecting me. "A parking ticket," she said without prompting. "Unpaid from January."

"I've never received a parking ticket," I said, so confident in that truth I expected her to apologize when she discovered a mistake had been made.

"In Monaca. Facing the wrong way. Five dollars plus a twelve dollar late fee." She handed me a yellow copy. "This jog your memory?"

"I've never seen this."

"The file says the constable's been working on this for quite some time. Ninety days delinquent makes you a scofflaw."

The address was where I had my car serviced. I told her I'd be right back.

The car dealer said he was willing to absorb the loss. He wrote out a check and told me that sometimes the guys servicing cars were in a hurry and maybe left my car where it didn't belong. He smiled and added that they were expanding their parking lot so cars wouldn't be parked on the street in the future.

The secretary took the check, but then she frowned. "Twenty-seven dollars and fifty cents for the constable's fee is also due."

"For a local phone call?"

"According to our records, the constable drove to your residence on two occasions. He logged several calls to Harrisburg."

My fragile patience snapped. "He drove to where I lived a year ago. He went back again when he already knew I didn't live there. He called Harrisburg instead of opening the phone book for my address."

"He performs his duties in a manner satisfactory to Magistrate Luberto."

Enough was enough, I thought. "I'm not paying for his incompetence."

A door opened and a man's voice intoned, "Do we have a problem here?"

"One of our scofflaws is becoming abusive."

"If he continues, call in a disturbing-the-peace."

"Just like that?" I said. "Raising my voice slightly is nowhere near disturbing the peace." The woman dialed the phone. The police, she said a minute later, were on their way. I sat and waited.

The policeman, when he arrived, looked as young as my students. He wore the uniform as if it were as unfamiliar as a graduation robe. "I understand you have a disturbance here," he said to the receptionist, who nodded toward me.

"I'm the guy who talks too loud," I said. I wondered if I should mention that I held a Ph.D. and was a college professor, but I counted on being calm and polite to serve me well.

The policeman motioned me toward the door. He walked me outside and said he was surprised because I was a professor at the local college and didn't look like anybody who needed to be arrested, a quick reminder about how in sync law enforcement works. I answered him in coherent, complete sentences sprinkled with polysyllabic words. He told me to forget it, that some people were touchier than others, and I thanked him and left.

I had bigger problems than unfairly owing a small sum of money to the county, but when I arrived home I filled my story with obscenities directed at the Magistrate and Constable who were Fascist assholes and fucking morons. My wife shook her head and put a finger to her lips. She was holding our ten month-old daughter, but our son, who was about to turn four, was somewhere nearby.

Beginning in July, I could collect unemployment compensation. I'd worked up a monologue on humiliation and embarrassment that I declaimed to my wife, but as the day when I would become eligible drew close, I put on a coat and tie and drove off to Beaver Falls as if I was about to begin a new job that just happened to be in a government building.

It was a beautiful summer day. The office was located on a residential street that was tree-lined and well-kept, as if somebody was softening the blow by not locating it downtown among the largely abandoned store fronts that led down the hill to the closed factories or uptown toward the soon to be closing mill.

The only women in the room were employees. In the summer of 1975, only men seemed to be out of work. Though I was the one applicant dressed as if I had a wedding to attend, none of the men looked shiftless or crazy or drunk. Nobody talked except when their turn at one of the desks or windows arrived. I filled out my application and answered a clerk's questions. Very shortly, I would begin to receive a weekly check that would continue to arrive for one year. The woman I was speaking with looked me over for a few seconds before telling me I wouldn't have to report to receive my check. All I had to go on as to whether this was unusual was her telling the two guys in front of me that they had to report each week to receive their checks in person.

She didn't ask me about my months-long search for another college teaching job. If she had, I would have told her I'd applied for fifteen college jobs and one high school position as Chair of an English Department, but had only one interview so far. That interview hadn't been on a college campus. It had been in a New York City hotel room and made me more despairing than hopeful. I had nine postcards thanking me for my interest while telling me the position had been filled. The rest of the places I'd applied to had been silent.

A week after receiving my first unemployment check, arriving home from a day in the park with my wife and two small children, I found a note tacked to my back door that read: "Because of your failure to complete payment of all existing, past due fines, I visited your residence today, 7/15/75, to serve a warrant for your arrest. Please be so advised."

I crumpled that note into a tight ball, but before I threw it away, I copied the address and waited until the following day to settle in front of the typewriter. I wrote a reasonable, educated note to Magistrate Luberto requesting a formal hearing. I explained the circumstances for which I was being persecuted in polite and correct language. I used my title of Doctor both at the end and, ready-made, on one of the return-address stickers my mother had bought for me the moment I told her I'd passed my dissertation defense. I attached a stamp to an envelope whose address I double-checked for accuracy in the phone book. "There," I told my wife. "It's time for at least a little bit of justice."

The unemployment checks arrived exactly on time, but as July closed down, I was in panic mode. For another month I could tell any potential employer my reason for leaving my teaching position was that it required obedience more than creativity. Framing that explanation in the right way, I could make myself sound ambitious rather than the arrogant, over-confident jerk I'd let surface with my superiors, but by September I'd be susceptible to even a cursory background check.

As August began, I received a phone call from a college in Michigan I'd applied to in June, so late in the hiring season that I thought they might be desperate. The man on the phone said they wanted to interview me, and I didn't hesitate to say I'd be happy to drive to their campus. "We sometimes meet our applicants half way," he said. "We could interview you in Detroit to save you some miles on such short notice."

My excitement dimmed. Sure, I lived near the Ohio border, but it was still Pennsylvania, and Detroit was about 300 miles away. How could that be half way unless it was just a figure of speech? I told him I'd let him know by the following day. I owned a United States Atlas, and I opened it to Michigan. I couldn't find the city. Not at first, at least. Not until I realized it was located in an insert that contained the Upper Peninsula because there wasn't room for the entire state according to scale.

I thought of blizzards and wolves and every other problem that went with what was essentially the same job I'd let slip away because I hated doing nothing but teaching the same two sections of composition over and over with no chance of that schedule changing in the foreseeable future.

The next day, as I waffled about having the nerve to turn down a possible job offer, I received yet another early August job opportunity phone call, and this one, though it was the high school job, at least didn't sound like a safety net. There was an on-site interview in upstate

New York. When could I be there? I chose three days from then to make it look as if I had options.

Two days later, I answered the door without thinking of anything but the good fortune of having an interview the following afternoon, and there stood Sam Stambaugh. He didn't produce a warrant. He asked if I'd be willing to ride with him to the Magistrate's office to get things taken care of once and for all. When he assured me I'd be having a hearing, I said I'd ride along. "You ought to have cleaned this thing up sooner," he said on the way over. "I'm surprised somebody with your education wouldn't see the sense of it."

Luberto showed up looking like somebody who'd just finished mowing his lawn. "We have the matter before us of $27.50 in constable's fees unpaid," he intoned. "And additional costs of the court to transport you to these proceedings. Are you contesting?"

I began as evenly and clearly as I could muster. "I sent you a written request for a formal hearing. I put everything in the letter."

"This office has received no correspondence from you," Luberto said, and then, as if he could read my mind, he added, "Did you make your request by registered mail?"

Anyone could see how this would end, but I soldiered on. "I mail hundreds of letters a year," I said. "Every one of them gets through. They're sent first class with the correct postage and a return address. It's foolproof."

"We have no letter," Luberto said, and I sensed Sam Stanbaugh shuffling closer.

"But you received it."

Luberto looked at Stambaugh as he said, "Are you questioning the truthfulness of this court?"

There was nothing for it but to go all-in. "You bet," I said.

"Do you have a copy?"

Stambaugh stood so close now I could feel his breath. "No," I said, self-identifying as an idiot.

Luberto seemed satisfied. "One of the two parties in this dispute is being dishonest. The court has no reason to lie. A total of $82.50 is due now. If you are unwilling or unable to produce payment at this time, I will direct Constable Stambaugh to transport you to the county prison to begin a five-day detention."

To save face, I told him to lock me up, but in the morning I had to be up and out of the house by 7:30 at the latest, and my bravado was extinguished by the time we arrived at the prison. Scofflaw in the face of authority was one thing; getting a professional job before all of my education and ambition crumbled was another.

My fingerprints were taken. Like millions of possible felons, I was "in the system." When the guard confiscated what I was carrying, I asked him for my contact lens case. I have to have that, I explained, and he was reluctant. "Use your call if you wanna," he said. "Explain your special needs to somebody else."

I played tennis regularly with a lawyer. I was even wearing shorts and a t-shirt he would recognize if we were meeting at the courts. I looked up his number. His response was brief. "You have a case. You'd probably win, but it will cost you more than you'd receive. You could paint yellow lines for all the no parking zones in the county, but you should get your wife to ante up before the Magistrate shuts off his phone for the night."

Never had such perfect sense seemed so readily apparent. I gave him my phone number so he could call my wife and tell her to pay up.

Shortly thereafter I was led down a hall lined with cells. Every cell had a couple of residents. Every prisoner was black. Not one of them said a word.

Downstairs was what appeared to be a rec room half-filled with cots. The rest of the space held a television set and a ping pong table and a handful of chairs. Every prisoner was white.

"What you bringing us?" one guy said.

"Scofflaw."

There was laughter all around.

"How much goddamned scofflaw we talking about?" the same guy asked when my escort had disappeared. I told my story. I included each of the tiny sums of money. The prisoners seemed fascinated and empathetic. "Ain't that just the fucking way the man works?" seemed to be the consensus comment. The room, as I quickly learned, was populated by repeat DUI offenders and failure to pay child support deadbeats. Each one of them wanted me to know how "the man had fucked him over for nothing."

The Pirates were on the television, but they were losing, and baseball seemed trivial. But the ping-pong table was available, and I picked up a paddle. During the next hour, until my wife showed up to drive me home, I won half a dozen games because I was the only person in the room who seemed to know what topspin could do to the ping-pong ball.

Just before midnight, we picked up our children at our neighbors' house. My wife accepted our daughter, and I carried our son back to the house. Neither of our neighbors asked a question. "What did you tell them?" I asked my wife.

"That you had a problem that was running late and you needed a ride."

"A problem?"

"What was I supposed to call it?"

"We're going on a trip to New York in the morning," I told my son. We'll wake you at seven. You can sleep in the car." I found one clean and ironed shirt in the closet. To get a head start, I hung it and a tie and a sport coat from a hook in the back of our car.

In the men's room of the McDonald's ten miles from my interview site, I put on my clean shirt and tie. I combed my hair, happy that I'd had the foresight to have my wife trim it two days before. It was as short as it had been in five years; without asking, she had halved the length of my sideburns.

Fifteen minutes later, because of the early August heat, I carried my sport coat inside the high school before I put it on, one more step toward acting like someone who had qualifications to be in charge of an English Department even though I was sure my one year of high school teaching and six credits of education courses made me the least qualified of the other ten current members to lead.

No matter. I was going to talk to my strengths. What I knew was, no matter whether students were bad or terrific, few of them could write. I went on about how I would design a curriculum built around writing. I added plans for a literary magazine and sending out PR to the media about student accomplishments when they entered regional and state-wide competitions. I was ready to make the school well known for writing, a model other schools would copy. I spoke as if I'd thought everything through with care. Hadn't I'd written an article about just those things that had been published a few months before in a journal that maybe three dozen school administrators had read?

The Superintendent of Schools nodded along. When I paused, he sat back in his chair and said, "I like having my male English teachers carry themselves like men because English teachers have to work with all kinds."

I didn't need an interpreter to understand that I'd passed one large section of my job test by the accident of heredity. I'd walked into his office at 6′2″, 210. My years as a tennis coach at the two-year college were on my vita. The conversation switched to sports and how I'd managed to occasionally come off the bench for a small-college basketball team. "Between you and me," he said before I was escorted to where the high school Principal waited to talk, "some of our male English teachers haven't earned the proper respect from their students."

The Principal, however, needed more than size and a history of sports. I took a detour to talk about rapport and large group discipline situations when he seemed on edge about those things not being part of the resume of a college teacher. I fell back on my one year of high school teaching, the job I'd had while I finished my Master's degree. I told him about study hall duty in the school auditorium, two teachers handling 200 bored and restless students. He started to nod the way the Superintendent had and let me move on to literature, reminding me that, for now, the curriculum emphasized reading and remembering because New York required students to succeed on a state-wide Regents Examination. I cited writers that I knew were safe choices and added a few contemporaries. I told stories about tests I'd taken full of spot passages to identify. When he told me that the test results for each teacher's students were published in the local newspaper, I said I welcomed the challenge.

My graduate education was never brought up. Not one question was asked about my research. Not one question was asked about the handful of stories and poems I'd published in the last two years. By the time the interview ended, it had been sixteen hours since I'd been released from jail, but nobody, for sure, had to know that, not even my children.

A secretary showed me around the school while the Principal and Superintendent discussed me. When I returned, the Principal gave me a school yearbook to help me get to know my colleagues. The Superintendent walked me down to his office for some paperwork. "We work fast when we think we're ready," he said. He made it clear that he liked the idea of having a teacher with the word "Doctor" in front of his name.

I walked out into bright sunshine and saw my wife and the kids sitting near the creek that ran across the street. The town looked absolutely picturesque. Sweat ran down my back and over my chest by the time I reached them, but all that was left of that day was the drive back home and extraordinary relief. By the time we reached our house, it would be nearly twenty-four hours since I'd been freed. Our neighbors would see us return if they were awake, maybe not worn out from staying up late with our kids the night before.

I'd spent not quite two hours in jail, a time very long or very short depending upon who you believe you are and what follows. In less than a month, I was going to be the head of an English Department. Now I had to become someone other than who I appeared to be to my former employers and the local judicial system. A scofflaw who had disregard for authority, a teacher full of untested theories and experience. Someone, in both cases, who could be easily dismissed.

Creekside

The babysitter lived in a large house with a yard bordering a creek that emptied into a river less than a mile away. That proximity worried my wife and me, but our son was the only child the babysitter, a woman recently separated from her husband, said that she watched for extra income. The house was large and clean, everything in its place in a way that suggested responsibility.

The arrangement worked well. For nearly two weeks, no matter my wife's erratic work schedule, the babysitter was waiting with our smiling son in her living room when I arrived after school. Our son even seemed happy when I dropped him off, no longer crying like he had at the former babysitter's apartment where he had been bitten twice by an older child.

Friday afternoon of the second week I parked, as always, where the driveway ended at a patch of worn grass near the back door. I knocked. Then I knocked again. While I waited, I noticed how full and deep the late-spring creek was running less than fifty feet from where I was standing.

At last, I turned the knob and the door, unlocked, swung open. Our son stood there smiling. I picked him up, hugged him, and called "Hello?" twice before I began to search the house, finding the babysitter asleep in an upstairs bedroom, sprawled in a way that made me think she could have been drinking.

The babysitter gathered herself and mumbled, "I must have dozed off for a minute." She didn't seem to recognize what the problem was. "He's two years old," she said. "He can't open the door."

"More than two and a half," I said, already walking toward the stairs. "He's opened doors before."

The babysitter followed me down to the kitchen where I put our son down at last. "Maybe at your house, but not here," the babysitter said. "He knows not to touch so there's no problem." I started to list disasters encouraged by a sleeping babysitter, all of them preceded by opening a door—falling down the cellar stairs, pulling cleaning products from under the sink, and loudest, drowning in a rain-swollen creek.

"That's extreme," the babysitter said. "He would never go near that creek."

While I counted out what I owed the babysitter, our son turned the knob and opened the door for us to leave. "Trust me, that's new," the babysitter said.

Before I had finished explaining how I wasn't bringing him back on Monday or any other day forever, our son ran straight to the car. "See that?" the babysitter crowed, as if that proved something. "See?"

Headlines

Bomb Threat Closes School

In the spring of 1980, a bomb threat was called in to the high school where I taught English. Less than fifteen minutes later, the building was emptied of students, the faculty close behind. The school, located between Buffalo and Rochester, had six built-in snow days in its calendar. In four of the five years I taught there, more were necessary, but that day, at 9:30, the streets were clear, the temperature was mild, and it felt like a holiday. Despite the small chance that the threat might actually end in destruction and even bodily harm, I had to admit it was exhilarating to be walking home mid-morning. Well before noon, I was informed by the school that the threat was a hoax.

First period was my free time slot that year. I used it to read the *Rochester Democrat-Chronicle* and listen to gossip in the faculty lounge. It was the worst time to have free period, the rest of the day, six classes and one large-group discipline situation, stretching, except for lunch, without a break, but on the day after the bomb threat, a colleague who taught remedial, small group classes in a trailer behind the grade school building, revealed that once roll was called and recorded, the day was legal. "Yesterday was better than an over-the-limit snow day," the teacher said, "because we're not making that one up."

"If that bomber calls again at nine o'clock, we're the luckiest teachers in the school," he went on. "We go home before we have to do anything but celebrate."

The other two teachers in the faculty lounge laughed cautiously, as if the principal might have the room bugged. I kept my mouth shut. I hadn't told anyone that I had been sending out applications to college English Departments since November, ready to put my recent PhD to work it was better suited for. The reading teacher didn't seem to notice. "He'll call again," he said. "He's a student who knows what's up. You can count on it."

My first class, second period, was for senior Non-Regents students, a designation applied by New York State. The students were unanimously marking time until they could leave school forever. There were two months left, the last marking period of their lives already begun.

One of my colleagues and I had talked the school into subscribing to the Rochester newspaper twice each week so we could use it to find stories that might encourage the students to take an interest in the world outside of their neighborhood. My section read it first, then folded it neatly and replaced it on a table for his section of senior Non-Regents to use during the following period. Sometimes we used the newspapers for two days straight if multiple stories excited the students. The day after the bomb threat, the headline on the first page of the local section of the paper was about our school.

The first student comment was "We're famous." The second comment was directed at me: "Admit it, teachers like a day off, too."

From then on, we talked about what might motivate someone to threaten the school and what consequences might follow until a minute before the bell rang. The class agreed that whoever it was would soon get caught because people who called in a successful bomb threat hoax would never be able to keep it a secret.

Students gathered their books and watched the clock. One girl, visibly pregnant, said, "I wish there was a real bomb and my old boyfriend was the one person who didn't leave when he was told to."

"But then he'd be famous," her friend said, "and that would suck."

The principal held a faculty meeting after school. He sputtered his outrage and guaranteed the hoaxer would be caught. He wanted everybody to have "ears on the ground" for "student scuttlebutt." The next morning, as first period wound down, the reading teacher looked at the clock and said, "Come on, bomber, do your thing."

Iran Gives OK to Family Visit

My English colleague and I approached the class in the same way. We called it Life Skills. The class read stories and took quizzes so the principal couldn't say we weren't teaching "English." But mostly, the class was given over to writing short essays on newspaper stories and role-playing life experiences that showed them they needed to read, write, and speak well enough not to be taken advantage of. We both knew that the students faced a state-mandated test in mid-June that they had to score 65% on in order to graduate. Their scores were our test, too, because we were judged on how many passed. The principal used our numbers for PR. He released them to the local paper like football scores. A "losing season" was unacceptable.

But it was still April, and that section I taught was concerned about other things—saving up for a car, working part-time, and above all, since two-thirds of the class of twenty-seven were girls, getting pregnant, being pregnant, or, in three cases, taking care of the babies they already had.

After five years of teaching at that school, I'd learned that late winter/early spring was pregnancy season for seniors. Aside from rare exceptions, those girls wouldn't deliver until late summer or early fall. It seemed as if they had spent Christmas break in bed with boys who pledged their love daily for two weeks in between looking at brochures for whichever branch of the Armed Forces they most wanted to join.

Currently, eight of those eighteen girls were pregnant. Two of the three who were already mothers had given birth the summer before; the other had only told me she had "a son." Since early March, every one of the current pregnancies had been signaled in class by a girl crying "for no reason." The other girls would alternate between consolation and congratulations. Half of the pregnant girls expected their boyfriends to stick by them.

By now the Iran hostage story bored them. When the discussion stalled, one boy closed it by saying, "Carter's a pussy. My dad hates him."

What they always wanted to talk about was Terry Fox, who had lost one leg to cancer, running across Canada. On April 12th, Fox had dipped his artificial leg into the Atlantic Ocean in St. John's, Newfoundland, and his Marathon of Hope had begun.

The class had read that story eagerly, how a police escort and a small crowd had witnessed the departure of Terry and his van. The students were fascinated by his equipment—eight pairs of running shoes, three extra legs, and various spare parts.

Though English classes met in that room throughout the day, there was a map of North America that scrolled down across the front blackboard. A week earlier, somebody had stuck a small gold star on the edge of Newfoundland. We were going to follow Fox across Canada, adding a star every week until the end of the school year. "Next fall he'll be close," the girl who stuck on the star declared. "I have a sister who will be in this class. She can finish the stars." The second star, though, touched the first.

I didn't blame them for falling in love with the Terry Fox story. It was way more hopeful than talking about the hostages in Iran, inflation, or Jimmy Carter's threat to boycott the summer Olympics. Rumor had it that one hostage was already dead, critically ill at the least, but the fanatics were keeping that secret. Near the end of the period, when we returned to the Iran situation, we discussed what might be done to successfully free the hostages, the students unanimously voted for a full-scale invasion.

Hostage Rescue Mission Fails—8 Killed

"Come on, bomber," the reading teacher said as the clock lurched toward the end of first period. Years before he rooted for another penalty-free day off from school, he had been the guy who had advised me never to use a sick day for being sick. "What's the point of a day off if you're sick and can't do anything?" he'd said. "Tough it out when you're feeling like shit. The day's wasted anyway. Use sick days for doing something you like."

Second period began without a bomb threat. Every student already knew what would be the headline. Everyone read past the front page without being asked, absorbing the details of how an attempt to rescue the American hostages from the occupied United States Embassy in Tehran was canceled by President Carter after two American aircraft collided on the ground. Eight crew members had been killed in the crash, several others injured. The military personnel had been airlifted out of Iran. They were all still reading when a boy slapped his newspaper down and said, "We left the bodies there. My father says that's never supposed to happen, not ever. He says it's Carter's fault because he's such a coward it rubs off on everybody."

The girl sitting beside him closed her newspaper. "My father yells at Carter when he's on the news," she said. "It's like Carter is my older brother the way he curses him."

One of the young mothers said, "My mom says yelling is a good thing. It means you still care, right?"

"She just wants you to do better," the first girl agreed.

"At anything, right? Taking care of my baby. Yelling when I have to."

Looking straight at me, the first girl said, "Yelling doesn't scare me. It's when you sometimes just stare at us the way my Dad looks before he says I'm worthless. Like you're out of caring."

Is Economic Embargo Enough?

The following week there was another phoned-in bomb threat. Like before, just after nine o'clock. The next morning's newspaper used two paragraphs in a sidebar summary of "Regional News" to summarize.

"It's not news when it happens again, is it?" a boy said. "It's just a small crime where they think nothing important happens because it's thirty miles from the city."

I'd expected disappointment, but before anyone else spoke, there was a fresh set of tears, this time from the girl who was new to the school, a near-stranger who had moved to town just after Thanksgiving. The girls showed the same empathy. Even the boys waited for a few minutes, none of them taking advantage to start a separate conversation while the girls who were consoled in late-winter provided comfort in mid-spring, hugs and tears and, nearly without exception, an invitation to the community of disappointment in fathers.

Before class ended, the crying girl raised her hand and asked me how old I was before I got married. When I said twenty-three, she said, "That sounds so old. I thought I could finish high school before I had a baby, but I'd never make it all the way to twenty-three. I'd be like forty when she was in high school. My mother's thirty-three right now. Like Jesus when he went back to heaven she says sometimes. Isn't that spooky?"

"Not when you're thirty-four," I said, but whatever cleverness that line had disappeared without a reaction when another girl broke in. "I bet you got married and she wasn't pregnant. Am I right?

"That's right."

"Wow," the crying girl said. "You two must have been really lucky."

"There's pills. And other choices, too, but they're the easiest."

I thought she was going to say she was ashamed to ask or her mother wouldn't permit it, but instead she said, "Aren't you afraid of hell?" as if bringing up birth control had never crossed her mind.

The period was nearly over, and there was nowhere to go except into controversy. When a girl who wasn't pregnant waved her hand, looking excited, I was happy to call on her. "I heard there's a McDonald's coming to town," she said. "It would be fun working there. I love how McDonald's smells, don't you?"

No one, the entire period, had commented on the embargo that was supposed to force Iran to capitulate to Carter's demands.

After school, at a faculty meeting, the principal announced, "The authorities believe they have a way to catch whoever it is. If there is another bomb threat call, we'll put an end to his fun. And there will be no mitigating circumstances that will affect appropriate punishment,"

On the way out of the meeting, the reading teacher poked me and repeated, "You know what mitigating circumstances are? They're what puts kids in front of me in the trailer."

I nodded, but kept walking.

"You know what I'm talking about," he said. "You have seniors. They never learn to read because they're too busy fucking."

Tito Dies

"Who's that?" was how the class began, followed by "Who cares about Yugoslavia?"

I scrolled the map down and someone added a new star. Everybody clapped, but the stars were forming a solid line that already was farther across Canada than Terry Fox. The girl who loved McDonald's said, "Wow, Canada is so big. This will take him forever."

Ten minutes late, the girl with "the son" walked in holding his hand. "Sorry," she said. "Issues. You know."

The other girls were unanimous in delight. "He's three," she said, anticipating the question.

"So's my youngest," I said, giving in to the moment. "He turned three last week."

"This guy will be four," she said, and because she was no older than any of them, I knew that everyone in the class, even the boys, was doing the math.

A hand went up, and the conversation switched back to news. A girl asked everybody to look at a short obituary because its header said the dead woman had lived in our town and worked at the Jello factory until it had closed. "They made Jello here," the student said, looking at the new girl. "We used to be famous. My grandmother worked at the Jello her whole life. My mother told me she grew up believing that's what she would do, too." The girl became animated, the class quiet. "Imagine that," she said, "being a little girl and already knowing what you wanted to do. It was like living in a town where Willy Wonka had his candy factory, and then it wasn't. She had to quit school when she got pregnant. They wouldn't let you go to class once you started showing back then, so I'll be the first girl in my family to finish high school."

She looked at me for a moment. "Another month, right?" she said. "Hardly any time at all."

Tito Buried

Half way down the front page was another headline that interested everybody more than additional news about Tito. The class was eager to talk about Mt. St. Helens, the volcano that was threatening to erupt, and especially about Harry Truman, the old man who refused to evacuate and always had something fascinating to say.

"I don't have any idea whether it will blow," he had told reporters. "But I don't believe it to the point that I'm going to pack up. If the mountain goes, I'm going with it. This area is heavily timbered, Spirit Lake is in between me and the mountain, and the mountain is a mile away, the mountain ain't gonna hurt me."

The students wanted to talk about that last part. They thought his contradictions were funny, but they loved his bravado. By now, he overshadowed Terry Fox.

"Why doesn't that guy leave?" was how discussion started.

Guesses came rapidly:

"He thinks he knows more than anybody else."

"He's an idiot."

"He wants to die."

"He doesn't want to move and be like a hostage stuck in some place where nobody thinks like he does."

Slasher Films Concern Experts

The class searched for a quote from Harry Truman to write on the side blackboard that nobody ever seemed to use. "You couldn't pull me out with a mule team. That mountain's part of Truman and Truman's part of the mountain."

"Current events are interesting now," the girl doing the writing said. "It's not just old men trying to be President. People like feelings way more than science."

When the class read that Truman received hundreds of letters, they decided to compose one and send it to him. "It will be practice for the stupid test we have to take in June," a good excuse, but then somebody found a review of a movie that had just arrived at a neighboring town's theater to talk about.

"*Friday the 13th* is low budget in the worst sense, with no apparent talent or intelligence to offset its technical inadequacies," she read out loud. "It has nothing to exploit but its title." Everybody started to turn pages to find what she was reading from. "Another teenager-in-jeopardy entry with six would-be counselors arriving to get the place ready and being progressively dispatched by knife, hatchet, spear and arrow, the murders telegraphed too far ahead to keep anyone in even vague suspense, and without building a modicum of tension in between."

"Modicum," a boy said. "What kind of jerk uses a word like that?"

"That guy's wrong," another boy said. "You'll see. It will be famous."

"My dad says movies like this have it right," the McDonald's girl said. "It's a metaphor. You have sex, you get pregnant, your life is over."

Miss South Carolina Crowned Miss USA

The authorities were right. The third bomb threat exposed the callers, two boys who, incredibly, were calling from the pay phone in the school lobby. "How dumb is that?" the reading teacher said. "We need smarter bombers. Different pay phones for each call, and we'd be back home again."

Only one girl wanted to talk about Miss USA instead of the bomb threat story, which was in the local section again and just two paragraphs long. No names were mentioned there, but everyone already knew the callers' identities. I'd had both students the year before. One had been in a Regents class, an excellent student until after the Christmas holiday. He began to be frequently absent. He failed every test. Drugs, classmates said in a way that revealed that it wasn't beer or marijuana, things they found amusing and exciting.

The other I'd had in a Non-Regents class, a boy who'd moved in during the year, skinny and unkempt and unable to do even the most basic work. He lived in a trailer, students said, something unusual in that school district. Everyone agreed they were an unlikely pair. "What's going to happen to them?" somebody asked right before the class ended.

Muskie Blast Soviets

Nobody opened their newspaper. Everyone knew that the trailer-boy had been expelled and the drug-addled boy was going to receive home schooling once his ten-day suspension had expired. "How does that work?" somebody asked. "He gets a prize for making those calls? Ten days of no school and then private lessons?"

"Because he's fifteen until school ends, they have to teach him."

"So, if any of us called in a threat, they'd kick us out for good?"

"Yes. And maybe prosecute."

"What if you hurt somebody? You know. And you were fifteen. What then?"

"That's different," I said, though I didn't know for sure.

One of the visibly pregnant girls waved her hand. "I was really scared that first time. What if I lost my baby because I was so scared? Would he still get tutored and even get to come back to school?"

"That's complicated."

"Exactly. Right? Complicated."

I looked from face to face as if I was waiting for somebody to raise his hand. "Yes," I said at last.

"Another Brick in the Wall," a boy said, and three students said "Exactly" in near unison.

"We should role play a trial," the girl said. "You have to be the judge who asks all the questions. Half of us could be the jury because anybody can be on a jury. The other half could be witnesses and defendants because anybody can have things happen to them."

Eruption Blots Out Sun, 7 Killed

"Harry Truman will be a fossil," a boy said as soon as he picked up his newspaper. "Ten thousand years from now somebody will dig him up and put him on display because he'll be so well-preserved."

And then everybody talked nearly at once for a few minutes before I quieted them down long enough for that boy to break back in. "Wouldn't that be the best way to die? All at once? He was already old, so why not die like that and be preserved instead of rotting away?"

"Like those people who die on Mount Everest," the boy beside him said. "They freeze and stay themselves forever."

"Not exactly," I said.

"But almost, right? Enough to stay looking like somebody instead of a box of bones in a hole."

Carter Tours Volcano

We were spending less time with the newspapers now, the state exam less than a month away. Though the class was considered Non-Regents, the test was labeled Regents Competency Exam, a suggestive name I was happy not to mention. If they failed, there was an opportunity to take it again in August, a motivation-killer I kept to myself.

The new girl kept her newspaper closed, but she raised her hand when I referenced the front-page headline. "My dad said he's sorry Carter didn't fall in."

Play Ball!

"What a dumb headline," a boy said. "They never stopped, did they? They just pretended they were going to strike and then everything got fixed."

"There's so many things to care about and the front-page picks baseball?" the new girl said, and nobody argued.

For the next three weeks, I would be showing them how their short essays would be evaluated and how points were assessed for their speeches. I would be explaining how, if they did well on essay and speech, they needed barely more than fifty per cent on the multiple-choice questions that covered reading comprehension, vocabulary, and grammar. No one would question my optimistic math. One more girl cried "for no reason."

We did trial runs on thesis statements, support, transitions, and conclusions. They wrote a five-paragraph essay three times a week and learned where points would be subtracted according to state-mandated rules. "Have an attitude," I said, "and then back it up."

"Show me," I repeated when trial-speeches began. "Make me understand using details about something you know best." Most of the class was terrified. There was a week of mumbling and shaking hands, but everyone gave three practice speeches, each a bit better than the one before, mastering the point-system for success. Everybody clapped for each practice speech.

The newspapers, some days, were not even opened. The Terry Fox map was given three more crowded stars. "Maybe you can come in this summer and add a few more to get ready for September," somebody said, but by then Terry Fox would stop running because the cancer that would soon kill him had returned, and I would be working at a college hundreds of miles away.

New Fossils Age Life a Billion Years

Immediately, two students pointed out that the headline couldn't be correct because the earth was only 6,000 years old, but no one else in the room even opened the newspaper on the last day of class. There were yearbooks to sign, something all of them agreed was more important than "Bible talk."

Three days later, everyone showed up to complete their Non-Regents English exam. All twenty-seven passed, most with scores between 65 and 75, but there weren't any additional rewards for a higher score.

Their results were published in the local weekly paper a few days after graduation—my name, including my title of *Dr.*, then the name of the class followed by 100%, the public version of a perfect score. Nothing was said about the makeup of the class, what the principal would call "their mitigating circumstances."

The Past Tense of the Census

In the census year, with three small children now, my wife sought part-time work, self-designed hours convincing her to canvas our county of farms and quiet, well-zoned streets. There were heads to count, assessment questions, and not every house, she soon learned, was welcoming. House trailers were rare and always alone, set so often on barely landscaped lots that she was surprised, this late afternoon, by one site's borders of high wooden fence, a lawn weed-infested, yet closely mown by somebody, she thought, who was taking whatever care he could, not a man who opened his door and stood naked to show whatever news he might possess could wait.

Once exposed, a man might be capable of anything, logic that hurried her to our car where she turned, keys posed to thrust, and saw the trailer door closed, driving home touched only by a familiar story during the year Jimmy Carter looked sad, as if he understood another sort of census would defeat him—hostages held in Iran, inflation, scarcity of oil—though we spoke nothing of that while our children scattered around our fenced-in back yard, twilight settling, our neighbor's Black Lab barking longingly at the gate as my wife began, hushed and intimate, to speak while we stood beside the deck rail so our children could see we were watching.

What did he say? I asked. *He was soundless.* What did he do? *He picked his teeth and spit.* How close was he? *Arms' length. Able to reach. I'm never counting him—is that a crime?* And right there her story ended as if she was willing to tear only one page from her notebook of murmured memory.

Carter is smiling now, benign with age. Though he must have more than such small horrors to tell, the country exposed and ugly, taken hostage and held for limitless ransom. That man, years ago, was surely naked as he watched my wife, a stranger, cross his cropped-weed yard. And surely, he had his chance to choose shorts and shirtless or call out "Just a moment" before fully clothed, choosing, instead, full-frontal exposure.

That evening, all we could see of our three children was movement. They appeared to be vanishing, about to no longer live in our house, my wife using the past tense of the census to say, "He was, he was" in a sentence stuttering, then gone dark.

More Unique

In English class, grades six through twelve, we learned and relearned the error of *more unique.* "Unique is unique," Mr. Sutton said throughout eighth grade. "One of a kind is one of a kind," Miss Price reminded us until tenth grade ended, hoping, perhaps, her translation would help the worst of us see the bad sense of our insistence.

The first time I read about a novel called *Gadsby* and how its author Ernest Wright typed his manuscript with the key for e removed as insurance, I thought nothing could be more unique than writing a novel without the letter *e*. Who would try such an extended lipogram? Who would examine it like a proofreader, looking for the stray *e* of the printer's error? Not many, it turned out—fifty copies were sold. It would take someone like a former colleague of mine, who read her student papers until she encountered the fourth mechanical or grammatical error. Immediately after that comma splice or typo or misspelling she'd draw a red line and stamp "You have exceeded the error limit set in the syllabus. I will read no further and you will receive no credit for the assignment."

My colleague kept her word. She also kept her enrollments low with this strategy, priding herself with taking a position on standards. For a year. For as long as it took the department to complete a self-study the students at that college should have read.

That study revealed she was the easiest grader in the department, for if the students avoided such errors altogether, she gave them an A. One error was a B, two a C, three a D.

What could be less unique than her system? Write in short, simple sentences. Use basic vocabulary you surely can spell. Be brief and reread for typos. Foolproof.

Ernest Wright and his novel *Gadsby,* I've learned, are less unique as well. There are other such books. Lope de Vega created five lipogram novels, varying the missing letter each time. Somebody else, incredibly, retold the *Odyssey* in twenty-six volumes, each without one of the letters of the alphabet. Thank the gods for q and x and z, that writer might have thought, and for the moment I'd claim "more unique" for that effort, turning in my paper to my old colleague and accepting a B.

Recently, I ran across a familiar item in a book detailing such one-of-a-kinds. A past president of the university where I teach was listed as the only college president who simultaneously coached the school's football team. In 1965, the coach quit and took his staff with him after seven straight losses, and, unable to find a replacement, the president devised strategies for two games, losing them both, but by respectable scores, some consolation, perhaps, for the awkwardness of becoming the make-a-wish coach.

I sat across from that past president once, appropriately, at an athletic banquet the day after a television station had done a story on me because of the unique combination of my being a writer, teacher, administrator, and tennis coach. "Probably not," was the phrase I kept to myself while the cameras rolled, but that past president had suffered a stroke and could no longer make his speech clear enough to recount his two games on the sidelines thirty years ago when I could have been a freshman on his team if I hadn't opted for something other than a contact sport.

No matter. A veteran professor explained to me that for years, pre-stroke, the past president told that story, self-deprecating and jovial, not claiming any credit for his accidental uniqueness. The president-coach nodded my way, not able to elaborate, and I didn't add anything to the athletic director's explanation about the publicity for my occupations, nothing unique at all without a list of qualifying adjectives.

Today, though, I'm across the state visiting West Aliquippa, being driven into town over its only entrance by another old colleague, this one a friend. *The Guiness Book of World Records* says West Aliquippa is unique, that of all the towns in the United States not surrounded by water, it's the only one with a single entry and exit. Crossing the wide swath of railroad tracks which bind it to the Ohio River, I continue to believe it.

In West Aliquippa, the streets are lined with the familiar housing of my childhood. I can imagine my grandparents sitting on these porches, and I consider asking my friend to park and wait while I enter one of the houses, emulating the explorers in Ray Bradbury's *The Martian Chronicles*. They land on another planet and find their families from home, their families from an idealized past, so they enter a nostalgia that proves fatal when the Martians reveal themselves. I think my visiting here will be as sentimental, full of listening to mill stories, church tales, and eating the fatty, gravy laden foods of childhood, another sort of fatal attraction.

This town is as small as the illusory one in Bradbury's novel. We roll slowly, block by block, but it's not long before we reach its end and pull over. My friend allows me to look for a few minutes at the empty space where the Jones and Laughlin steel mill had once stood.

"Well?" he says, and I know he thinks he's given me a subject.

"It's an airport," I say, "for a third-world country."

"Exactly," he answers, and I can tell I've estimated runway length reasonably well. My friend has a pilot's license. He's taken off and landed in fields like this. The mill had been enormous, sprawling for miles along the river. That it had shut down wasn't surprising. Somebody had drawn a line after the maximum number of errors allowed by industry. Somebody had refused to read further and declared failure, nothing at all unique except everything is gone—furnaces, flues, checkers, boilers, stacks, and every piece of scrap metal and bit of slag.

Between the mill and the tracks, it was like living on an island here, but now I'm convinced I could leave West Aliquippa by plane. Or, more likely, by foot, not having to manage the railroad tracks, which are fenced off, not having to climb anything, just crossing the length of this field where surely no one would stop me. Exiting miles from here, leaving behind this odd emptiness which seems to demand so explicitly to be filled in.

Like a blank book, one of those leather-bound volumes that are sold as joke or invitation, three hundred empty pages to thumb through. In 1970, when I lived near here, when I passed West Aliquippa weekly, somebody published *The Nothing Book* and found himself being sued for plagiarism by the publisher of an earlier set of blank pages called *The Memoirs of an Amnesiac*. The defense was "blankness is in the public domain," and though such cases drift out of the news, I think that strategy must have worked or else the plaintiff's lawyer discovered that another identical volume, *Essay on Silence*, had been published in 1898.

Now, I'm gazing at the quack grass and thistle, the milkweed and narrow leaf plantain, expecting the steel mill to emerge like the camouflaged imagery in those 3-D paintings I've stared at in the mall, waiting for dragons or dogs or one enormous eagle to lift into sight.

There are books filled with these pictures now, coffee-table artifacts replacing art and photography with the easy "oh" of the more unique. A salesman, once, told me to turn the pages slowly, to stare carefully at each. After the images lift from the page, he said, you'll see what the story is about.

It's 3-D without glasses, the *trompe l'oeil* of computers if we transfix ourselves. You enter the picture, the enthusiasts claim, and the artistry rises. Like toxins in this landfill. Like the untethered promises of developers.

WILL BUILD TO SUIT, it says on the signs posted at intervals by the company which now owns this land. So far, apparently, no one has thought of anything suitable. It seems more likely for the town itself to be leveled, everything three-dimensional flattening to the first-glance nonsense of a 3-D painting or a hopeless EEG, the families who live here debating whether or not to pull the plug on life supports.

In another area of the country where I've lived, a city added an exclamation point to its name in order to change its image. Hamilton, Ohio, became Hamilton!, one step toward the more unique of silly hope. It languished in urban decay despite the punctuation mark—before and after, Hamilton made the least livable cities list for Ohio.

Nearby, the town of Midland can no longer support a public school system. So far, that failure is unique in Pennsylvania, though West Aliquippa must be thinking about tax base and physical plant and the costs of teacher salaries. This year, the school district which accepted the state aid and tuition income from the students without a school has chosen to refuse them. Economics. Discipline. Race. Choose one or all of the above, but the only offer to accept them is from an Ohio district. More unique, I think, and a loop through the streets of Aliquippa proper shows Midland enlarged by all the familiar multipliers of neglect, despair, and fear.

In 1970, while I finished grading thousands of pages of student writing, reading through each of them twice no matter how many errors they contained, some of my students who lived in Aliquippa wrote about race wars they faced. J&L had overseen housing for many of its employees, setting them up in developments constructed along ethnic and racial lines. For instance, Plan 11 was black; another plan was Italian. There were occasional shootings, frequent threats and skirmishes. Twenty-five years later I don't ask my friend to tour any of those plans. We keep to the main street where the neutron bomb of abandonment has exploded.

The sentimental illusions by which we grow attached to what we build—like the J&L plant, believing in its importance, that size and productivity somehow represent us. The Salem Church Dam, on the Rappahannock River in Virginia, was 194 feet high and 8,850 feet long, large enough for the importance of a listing in the *Encyclopedia Britannica*. Until 1988, when it was deleted, someone discovering it was designed in 1944 but never built.

My old colleague with the red pen would have given the writer of the paragraph on the Salem Church Dam an A. No grammatical or mechanical errors there—you can check by finding an old edition of the *Britannica*. So easily, geography is altered. Less than an hour's drive from here is a waterslide park where the Homestead Steel Works once stood. The largest steel mill in the world, I was told, when I toured it in seventh grade. I remember the hard hat, the open hearth, and the catwalks. I can't call up anything about the workers or the guides, and this afternoon I don't see anyone who looks as if he ever trusted industry to build his house or secure his future.

Finally, we cross over the river to Ambridge, more steel mills, some of them operating. From this side of the river, from a town we can enter and leave in dozens of ways, the absent mill is more disorienting. The emptiness seems larger from farther away.

"Give this place fifty years," my friend says, and you'll need an historian to place it." And then he tells me the enrollments on the campus where we taught together have dropped by 50%, that 25% of the faculty have been furloughed. "For starters," he adds, his tone full of bulldozers and planned implosions.

In 1969, the year I took the job that introduced me to the colleague who refused four errors, one other writer produced a book which contained nothing but hundreds of pages printed with the letter i. He said it was an assault on the tyranny of words, using everything omitted from Volume Nine of the *Odyssey* lipogram.

Something like the 3-D artwork when nothing lifts from the page. Something like the special effects of blocking part of a camera's lens, filling in the images later.

So many times I've watched films where I know the actors have delivered their screams to the nothing of a matte. The monsters are added afterward, but those actors must have some idea about what is so terrifying. So they can open their mouths for shrieking. So they can take in air, preparing for a horror the director assures them will be more unique.

Specificity

Cause of death unknown. Had never been fatally ill before.
—Death Certificate, 1880s

Until I was twelve, worn out and God's will were the reasons my relatives died, my mother speaking like a doctor, citing visual evidence or unknowable matters of faith as if each were a diagnosis of disease.

In the King James edition of medicine, the self-help my grandmother relied on, there was the finality of dropsy, the chronic palsies, what Jesus cured, like leprosy and possession, the devil imbedded in the flesh like ticks.

Before she was born? People died from convulsions and fever, from infancy, age and tissick, the collective name for killers that came with coughs, as frequent as smallpox and grip of the guts, what the dying did, at last, when their digestion failed.

Approximation. Guesswork. Less of that now, the x-ray showing the shadow that will kill us, the blood sample spilling numbers that count us out, each tremor specific, ten thousand names exactly right, pinpointing each particular way to die.

Amyloidosis, for instance, how one friend, this week, has gone. And now, after memorial, after an hour of tributes about his poetry by writers who traveled hours to eulogize and loving anecdotes by family and friends, I sit with my wife who orders a glass of Chambord for a small, expensive pleasure in a well-decorated room, the possibility of happiness surprising us in the way hummingbirds do, stuck in the air, just now, outside this window, attracted to the joy of sweetness despite the clear foreshadowing of their tiny, sprinting hearts.

The Face-Blind

1

Once, discovering a crying child in a department store, I knelt to ask that girl the lost and found questions, her name, her address, and who had mislaid her in Gimbel's, a store that featured thirteen floors of merchandise.

Back then, toys were above everything but furniture, but we were on the first floor with perfume, cosmetics, jewelry, and well-dressed saleswomen who offered samples. Security, like her grandmother, was somewhere else, and when she clutched my hand, the nearby escalator so strongly suggested how easily something awful could happen that I half-expected an abduction alarm.

The tiny wisps of sprayed scents made the air seem funereal, the shoppers mostly old women who had driven to the city since World War II, so few of them by then the store was rumored to be going bankrupt. But suddenly, in Gimbel's, no one hailing that girl or me, not even when we approached the gilded, outside doors, I watched our reflection coming toward us and briefly recognized the dreadful alternatives to a common scene.

2

I warned my daughter, when she was seven, about not paying attention to where I was in a one-story department store that was spread out as an anchor store at the end of a Buffalo area mall. Three times in fifteen minutes. And then, when she ran off to look at toys in an adjoining aisle without me, instead of cautioning her for a fourth time, I slipped behind a pillar and watched her from hiding. It took nearly a minute before she looked around and saw that I was gone. I watched her nearly spin as she searched. For a few seconds, her face appeared to be blank, and I waited until she looked terrified before I stepped out when her back was turned and walked up to her as if nothing had happened.

3

Recently, a woman from Pittsburgh has revealed she is unable to recognize faces. Her daughter's teacher. A friend from church. The wait staff person who has just visited her restaurant table. Her daughter, seven years-old, prompts the names of neighbors, reminds her which of her friends have arrived for sleepovers. Like a bride receiving guests, she's taught herself to smile. A wonder we recognize anyone, she says, so much we have in common. According to the article in the newspaper about her, the condition she has is called prosopagnosia.

4

While I taught near Buffalo, I bowled on Friday afternoons with public school teachers like myself who needed to drink and drive a sixteen-pound ball into the pocket to feel better about another week of large group discipline situations—cafeteria duty, study hall, or a room full of in-school suspensions. My students ranged in age from fifteen to eighteen, college, work, or trouble bound, some of the girls so beautiful I trained myself to look over their heads to where I needed to concentrate on the sluggish and bored.

In early March, two of those bowlers were put on paid leave for alleged misconduct. Sixth and third grade, they taught, those men married like I was, with daughters, but by the end of the school year the one who photographed his eight year-old students found a new job teaching fourth grade in a school district an hour away because the principal commended his teaching in a letter for his file, passing him on like rumors because he hadn't touched those girls or asked them to undress, the photos explained as a sentimental hobby.

5

In the news, once, the story of a nine-year-old girl's unusual death. Because she needed to be taught a lesson, she'd been forced to keep running for three hours. For stealing candy. For being selfish. Her grandmother prodded her and screamed, making sure she didn't stop jogging in place, and apparently, she didn't until she collapsed into seizures and died like some unprepared marathon runner "hitting the wall."

The girl who died was on life support for a few days. She was so dehydrated her sodium level fell below what sustains life. The grandmother, the reports say, worked her over like a drill sergeant while her stepmother, within earshot and sight line, took care of her own three-year-old.

6

One night, when she was nine, our daughter screamed. When my wife and I opened her door, she was standing on her bed, her pajamas pressed against her body. A man's face had been at the window, she said. He wore a Phillies hat and he looked like a Halloween pumpkin. My wife calmed her down while I went outside to where I found a paint-splattered cinderblock that man had left behind, inviting us to check the garages of our neighbors to identify similar splatters on things stored in one of them. Or maybe, I thought, a supply of cinderblocks kept by a man who lugged them around the neighborhood as ladders while looking for windows where the drapes were open.

Years later, my wife told me the man who bought that house from us when we sold it had confessed to raping "his girls" in that bedroom where our daughter slept from ages six to ten.

7

Empathy is often said to be the ability to imagine yourself in someone else's place, understanding their feelings and desires, to, in the end, experience an appropriate emotional response. Just as often, I've noticed, the definition declares that empathy is the cornerstone of morality.

8

After we moved, the distance to our new home less than a mile, my wife and I would occasionally walk back to that house where the never-captured Peeping Tom had spent at least one night at the window. In less than a year the new owners took out the hedges along the edge of the property and replaced them with a fence. They dug out the shrubbery that nearly surrounded the front porch and left it bare. The yard filled with a litter of toys. "It looks terrible," my wife said, and I agreed. It was hardly recognizable, as if we'd never lived there.

9

That child I found in Gimbel's stopped whimpering after a short while. She clutched my hand. We finished half a circuit around the first floor before I saw where a set of offices were located. An employee in one of them said he would be happy to broadcast the name of the child's grandmother.

10

A man I knew in upstate New York told me how, at Niagara Falls, a woman he'd never seen before bent down to say to his young daughter, "What a darling you are," then followed those words quickly with "Want to see?" while she lifted her and swung her high. He thought, at that moment, the woman was the one person who would throw a child over the railing, and then, he was just as certain she was one of a few who would steal a child, who would flee into the crowd where she had accomplices who would pass his daughter like a relay baton while she disappeared among thousands of families because she carried a coat to wear over her distinctive purple sweater. He rushed at that woman, tore his daughter from her arms, and she cursed him as if he was a soldier assigning her child to a boxcar.

At the time, I thought this man was someone who exaggerated, someone who embellished stories to make an impression. "What did the woman look like?" I said, and the man shrugged.

"I have no idea," he said. "All I remember is that purple sweater."

11

Shortly after we moved to our new house, my wife and I walked the nearby highway where a man, we'd read in the newspaper, had thrown his daughter in front of a truck. We watched headlights approach from both directions. We gauged the speeds from the limit of forty-five to excesses of sixty or more. To get to a convenience store, we crossed the highway during breaks in the traffic. After we left the store, while we were waiting to cross again, I placed my hands on her back and said, "Imagine."

"What's wrong with you?" she said as lights came from both sides like testimony.

12

Prosopagnosia is a word I've never encountered before, yet when I investigate it online, I discover dozens of sites—questions from those who believe they're living with this condition, blogs from the self-proclaimed, jargon-filled medical tracts. On one of those sites I log on to a test to determine whether I recognize fear, anger, and joy in faces, whether those emotions reveal themselves to me in the faces of samples. Which doesn't seem to be a test for prosopagnosia, because anyone who fails to distinguish the emotions exhibited by the expressions presented wouldn't really see the humanity in a face at all.

13

Because I write biweekly columns for the local paper, my wife and I study its opinion page, especially looking for letters to the editor that react to what I write. She was the first to see the letter from the man who had raped three girls from three different families, apologizing from prison, acknowledging that his cellmate had written the letter for him as he dictated.

He used the word "molested" as if he was whispering in church. Both my wife and I, because all of those girls were younger than nine, vowed never to forgive, ready to remember like families who inherit vengeance.

An elementary school sits almost directly across the street from our house, reminding us five days a week about the size and shape of second and third and fourth grade, what we believed he still wanted as he dictated, "I hope and pray for them to heal." As if God would intervene, sending heaven's Red Cross to the country of damage.

Shortly afterward, at the school playground, I watched other peoples' girls while shame surrounded my eyes like gnats. I'd told my wife I hoped the inmate secretary would think to shorten penitence with a belt around the throat. She said she was trying to imagine the penmanship, the lines and loops. "It had to be clumsy," she said. "It was probably printed."

I kept to myself how I was sure the letter had been written on paper torn from the kind of tablet I carried home from grade school, passing pairs of girls who always dawdled, busy talking until one turned up a driveway and the other cut across a wooded lot to save herself three blocks of walking home alone.

14

The stepmother of the girl who was run to death was nine months pregnant when the girl died. She gave birth shortly after, conjuring in me the word "replaceable." A videotape from the dead girl's school bus had recorded the grandmother declaring to the driver, "I gonna run her till she can't run no more" just before she initiated the punishment she thought was appropriate.

15

Our daughter will have two daughters of her own. They will live in California, and one night she will call to tell us one of her paintings has been rented by the producers of the television series *Californication*. She sounds excited, but we don't subscribe to the channel that is showing the series. The painting, my daughter explains, is in David Duchovny's bedroom, just watch when you get the chance.

When we rent the series from NetFlix, we discover that the painting doesn't appear in episodes one or two, but there are occasional glimpses of a nude woman rising from Duchovny's designer sheets. And though our daughter has told us the painting is in episode three, I still follow those bodies past a wall of unfamiliar art. Soon, because he fucks a succession of women in that bed, his teenage daughter often nearby, she, too, sees those women naked, entering like a maid, all of them in that bedroom with my daughter's painting in Los Angeles where my daughter lives with her daughters, eight and five, who had run naked, two summers before, under the sprinkler in our yard.

I fast-forward through each external shot, hurrying toward my daughter's painting in David Duchovny's bedroom, the naked woman in episode three a creative writing student like ones I now teach, nineteen or twenty, sliding one step to the side so I can see the chairs suspended in the tumultuous blue sky of my daughter's rented painting on either side of that girl's bare shoulders. She talks and talks until, at last, she turns into profile, her breast the focal point of that artless scene, the painting completely exposed, half of the dark chairs silhouetted by the faint light my daughter allowed behind that storm of identical chairs in David Duchovny's bedroom.

16

My wife and I eventually learned from the newspaper that the man who bought our house raped each daughter at an earlier age than the one before. In order to have privacy, that bedroom where our daughter slept, where, I'm sure, those girls must have slept as well, had two doors that had to be locked. Surely, over a period of years, the mother would try one of those doors when she noticed her husband and one of the girls had vanished. She might even have taken to her tiptoes at that window used by the pumpkin-headed man.

"What kept those three girls from screaming?" my wife said. "How could they stay living in that house after he abused them? How could they stand to see him every day?"

"They probably learned to look right past him," I said. "You know, the middle distance or something like that."

"I don't believe that," she said. "And why didn't we recognize who he was when we sold our house to him?"

"I didn't look," I said.

My wife frowned. "That's just like you," she said. "Never noticing anything important. I bet you couldn't identify him if he walked into our house.

17

When I look up articles on empathy, I find a consensus that reads something like this: *Empathy is important in the development of a moral sense, a person's beliefs about the appropriateness or goodness of what he does, thinks, or feels.*

18

The sixth-grade teacher who bowled with me was eventually fired. During that spring, that man's daughter listened five days a week to my lessons on grammar, writing, and literature for the New York Regents Exam she'd pass in June, all semester babysitting for my three children, ages three to eight. Her father would be watching television when I walked her to the door after midnight, concentrating, most Saturdays, on *Chiller Theater* even when she said, "Hello." Two or three times I glanced at the aliens or zombies before I turned and left, not saying a word about the woman hired as his substitute or how no one took his place at bowling, his average minus ten used to compute his team's score each Friday, that number steady as a pulse propelled by machine until the league season ended.

During the summer that man quietly moved without announcing where. The third-grade teacher took his photographs to a school near Rochester. It was a time when Polaroids appeared slowly, so he would have had to watch light and shadow developing into a girl's body as he counted the necessary seconds, saying, "Yes, good, perfect, and thank you" when the image, at last, showed itself complete.

19

In that Buffalo area mall, among all those toys, there was such joy in my daughter's face as she saw me, I could barely stand myself, sick with recognizing an evil selfishness in myself.

20

When we visited in December of the *Californication* painting, our granddaughters slept over with us in the apartment we rented. One morning I convinced them to write and illustrate books of their own.

The cookie in my five-year-old granddaughter's self-illustrated book had long hair cut into bangs so much like hers I said, "The gingerbread man is a girl," but she explained he was wearing a wig. Like it always does in these stories, her cookie escaped the kitchen to run and play, but on the last page that gingerbread man was trapped inside the mouth of a scarlet fox, the wig gone in the final picture, lost, perhaps, in the struggle.

When I asked why he was smiling as he was being swallowed, she said, "Because he only has one face."

Her older sister drew twelve pages about a princess who needed to be saved. She was locked in a red-brick tower for a dozen sunny days, her hair tightly curled and long, but nowhere near what would welcome a prince to climb. One line per page, her princess sang an abridged "Over the Rainbow." Bluebirds dotted every clear sky. Lemon drops sparkled, then faded, but as the book ended, the prince, arriving on horseback, applauded but didn't dismount.

"What's next?" I asked.

"The rest of the story," she whispered, "is a secret-secret."

Later that day, my daughter, thirty-seven by then, volunteered that giving birth introduces the worst fear we can possibly know. As an illustration, she told me a story of her own. "Remember when I rode around for a few months, the year I was sixteen, in David Dixon's fast, expensive car?"

"Vaguely," I said, not telling her that I couldn't even remember who David Dixon was.

"Then you remember that he killed his next girlfriend," she said. "And he was just driving her a couple of miles to the movies."

I knew she meant me to understand this was about her daughters, five and eight, the probabilities of danger they're facing as they grow up, but then she leaned toward me as if those girls were eavesdropping. "I found out David Dixon's dead, too. On the internet when I looked him up. He died in another country, one of those places you've never heard of where nobody travels."

As if he had been a criminal, I thought. As if he had been disposed of.

21

The last day of our visit I gave each girl a piece of thin red cellophane cut into the shape of a fish. "A miracle fish," I told them. "It tells your fortune if you hold it in your hand for a minute."

They watched the miracle fish swim on their palms until the cellophane curled into *fickle, false,* and finally, lying still, *trustworthy.* Despite the novelty, their futures looked to be as unsurprising as the stories on their collection of Disney DVDs

In the morning, I hugged those girls goodbye and flew two thousand miles into winter.

22

Once, after a newspaper opinion piece of mine lamented the proliferation of child pornography on the Internet, a man sent me three emails, the first of which detailed his desire for young girls. He said he lived in Virginia, and he wanted to leave his wife for girls like the *littles* whose photos he collected.

Attention-getting, how willing he was to reveal himself a second, then a third time, increasing the chances of a prison sentence if I passed his notes along to the police. I remembered his emails each time the evening news carried a story connected to his explicitly detailed desires, driving me outside to dilute that memory with walking fast like I did, this week, when I heard about one more man arrested for storing child photos, unwittingly sharing with somebody whose job it is to pose each day as a preteen.

During my last such walk I wished that my temporary correspondent had turned out to be a policeman baiting like-minded men to reciprocal sharing of secret thoughts. I followed the approaching stratus clouds into the orange and scarlet of a late winter sunset, how they split the deep tangerine from the blue-going-violet during twilight's beautiful cruelty. Each hidden rustling sounded like words of dark, prophetic purposes, and I remembered that not one word that email pervert had sent me mentioned a characteristic of a child's face.

23

When my children were young, the milk carton that often sat on the table during meals always featured the face of a missing child. "Have You Seen Me?" its caption read, and those faces reminded me to be thankful even as my children yammered their petty complaints.

Eventually, milk cartons stopped showing lost children, but now those missing children's faces show up inside my income tax instructional booklet. I turn the pages, looking at each child, and all of them seem hopelessly lost. How are they chosen from among the thousands who are painfully eligible?

There are computer projections now of how those children, some of them lost for five or even ten years, would look in the present. My eyes shift from the photographs to the computer images and back again, searching for how facial features have been transformed. After a few minutes, I try not to imagine what most missing children end up looking like.

24

Some things need to be impossible.

No one recognizing a child so vulnerable to abduction from a failing department store.

A child run for three hours while no one recognizes her condition is nearing death.

A mother, her daughter there to coach her, searching, without recognition, the mug book of the everyday for the identity, not only of acquaintances, but also of those she loves.

No one recognizing that three sisters were being repeatedly raped by their father in my daughter's former bedroom.

How selfish I am to think a location I'm familiar with makes it worse.

Each blessing is lace. In Gimbel's, at last, a woman recognized her granddaughter's trusting face.

The Old Phrases

Billie Holiday's 1944 recording of "I'll Be Seeing You" was the final transmission sent by NASA to the Opportunity *rover on Mars when its mission ended on February 13, 2019.*

At the Center

My father's friend Harry, a man whose memory has perished before him, says, *Are you from the neighborhood? Are you here to take me home?* My father adjusts his pillow. *You're petered out,* he says. *Get yourself some shut-eye,* relying upon his old phrases for comfort.

As if he has dropped suddenly into sleep, Harry slumps in his wheelchair, but my father, instead of reaching for Harry, lays a hand on my arm. He keeps it there, his lips silently forming the measured count of a boxing referee. At seventeen, Harry stirs and sits upright.

Can I trust you? Harry says. *Can I trust you?* And when my father nods, he quiets. We shuffle. We wait. At last, Harry gnaws one word from the thick bone of his past. *Abyssinia,* he says. *Abyssinia,* as if an exotic-sounding ancient name would unlock our encrypted identities. Soon, my father pauses in the doorway to wave. *Abyssinia,* he calls to silence while I wait in the hall.

On the Road

Anymore, my father says, as I drive us to the cemetery, *none of my friends knows beans.* When I miss a turn, he sighs. When I turn into a wide driveway to correct myself, he stiffens and holds his breath until we're realigned. I slow for the gated entrance, turn in between the pillars embossed with crosses. My father opens his window and inhales. The early spring clouds over us as I slow to barely moving and ask about his friend's secret word. *Abyssinia,* my father says. *It was a country once.*

As I search for the pair of junipers I use each year as a landmark, my father says, *Abyssinia, say it fast. I'll be seeing you. Harry and I were just kids back then. There was a version by Sinatra.* He drifts into his own rendition. Softly, in his threadbare bass, he carries the tune through wistfulness as if it were a gravely injured body.

In the Cemetery

This will be the day my father fails to find my mother's grave. The old phrases follow while we search. The promised cold front wind carries the flurries of a Western Pennsylvania late March, flakes that go to water when they touch the landscaped earth, creating a damp pointillism of where we walk.

I know we are close. There is time enough not to help. Back and forth my father paces while I watch the nearby woods at the cemetery's border. I can tell he is using his foot prints in the wet grass as a guide. Three twenty-yard loops, just over a minute, take him to the plot.

When, at last, we lay our flowers beside her name, my father stumbles into silence. The day, by now, is full of the hum and whistle of devotion just out of reach. I imagine a tune for the present while we wait for the necessary words to embrace us. The old phrases clasp their hands and lower their heads. They recall my mother's mouth repeating them throughout each day, how she relied on them for the selective memory of her final years. Shuffling in place, they begin: *This language or none, for you will have no other.*

HARRISBURG

Sparklers

1

In late May, after baseball and the blasts of complimentary fireworks that opened nearly overhead, the pedestrian bridge to Pittsburgh, temporarily closed, compresses our crowd of late-night walkers. Someone next to my family mentions the latest terror, children and their mothers pierced by an explosion of glittering spikes after a pop star's concert in England. Faces of young girls illuminate two nearby phones. Ahead of us a father believes his arms have invented safety, yet somewhere, he must recognize, terror dreams our bodies as it decides the exact address for delight. The river's cruise ship passes beneath us, its decks packed with prom goers. The water reflects a swirl of pinwheels; a vendor ignites a fistful of sparklers.

2

For seven summers, the evening of the Fourth of July, I wrote my name in the air with a sparkler. Sometimes I circled them into brief, eclipsed suns or simply threw their violent lace into an arc that spiraled sparks to our lawn. Always, July 5th, I had to find every sparkler gone out and dropped the night before. Up and back, I paced our yard along the narrow paths the mower took. If there was even a hint of leftover nub on a wire, I tried to light it, but none ever burst into sparks. I threw away those wires and never once thought to learn what a sparkler was made of.

3

A sparkler is usually made from a wire coated from one end with a mixture of metal fuel, an oxidizer, and a binder. The most commonly used wire is made of iron and is most often coated in aluminum and magnesium for a yellow/white glow. The fuel is charcoal and sulfur, as in black powder. The binder can be sugar or starch. Mixed with water, these chemicals form a slurry that can be coated on the wire. Once dried, it is a sparkler, some as large as three feet in length in order to burn for several minutes to produce a long-lasting effect. They are non-poisonous if sucked on, but poisonous if eaten, causing gastrointestinal symptoms.

4

Sitting beside my son, I once watched a videotape of the beginning of a rock show at a Rhode Island club called The Station. The room in which a crowd was packed to hear a band called Great White looked so eerily familiar, it could have been one of the clubs I'd watched my son play lead guitar in for the previous three years. I remembered only "Once Bitten, Twice Shy," the band's biggest hit, but my son and I were paying attention to the pyrotechnics they were using, surges of sparks ascending as they began playing. "This is real bad," my son said, just home from touring in most of the venues Great White had played in the weeks leading to this show. He sounded thoroughly spooked. "Using pyro in places like this is crazy," he said, and watching that film, I couldn't argue. Those white-hot sparks set the back wall on fire, the flames running up to the low ceiling and spreading rapidly. "Somebody fucked up bad," my son added as the camera, seconds later, shut off. "Even you would know not to use it. There's no way you can miss the danger."

5

Typical pyrotechnics are made from flammable materials such as nitrocellulose and black powder or a mixture of fuel and oxidizer. A plug placed at one end of the container with a small orifice, called a choke, constricts the expulsion of the ignited pyrotechnic compound, increasing the size and aggressiveness of the jet.

6

When I was five years old, there was a fire in the back room of the bakery my father had purchased less than a year before. "Sparks from an electrical short in the old blue refrigerator that came with the place," my father said. "Hot enough to catch something that burns and there you have it, the place up in smoke." The fire was contained, but it took six weeks to make enough repairs to the back room and the roof to reopen. All of that work was done in the middle of winter. For nearly all of those six weeks the blackened refrigerator sat in the snow behind the bakery. In late January, he baked a cake for a small celebration of reopening. My mother placed one small sparkler candle in the center, and I watched until it went out, wishing for more.

7

I've learned that four-inch cake sparklers burn for about thirty seconds. For birthdays, some cake sparklers are shaped as numbers. Heart-shaped sparklers are sometimes offered as favors for wedding guests. To ignite those sparklers, the guests need to light them at the top where the heart creases in. Most often, the guests are given elongated, sparklers to light and hold while the newlyweds pass by. Those wedding sparklers are advertised as "dazzling," "brilliant," and "unforgettable."

8

Witnesses describing the bomb explosion after the pop concert in England were consistent. First, the red-orange flash, then the ear-splitting boom, then the bodies falling to the ground before a plume of smoke wafted over the crowd. More than one survivor said, "All this sort of debris and embers came floating from the roof."

9

I ran the Great White video again, this time remembering how I watched my son play, early in his career, from the privacy of a side room filled with piles of flammable trash, a room with exactly one way in and out. Watching closely, I checked to see which member of the band first notices the flames. It looked to be the guitar player I knew was dead. As if he was following my eyes, my son said, "It makes you think."

10

A pyrotechnic engineer usually has an undergraduate degree in chemistry or physics, followed by further training in pyrotechnics. Pyrotechnic engineers might work for firework companies or sporting arenas. Because safety is a factor in their work, some states require a licensing exam.

11

When I was eleven, Mrs. Cellander, our next-door neighbor, watched, like I did, a great sparkling puff of newspaper lift and float into her cherry tree from the burn barrel I was tending near where our back yards bordered. She screamed and swore and reminded me I was a careless idiot who deserved to be burned if that tree was damaged. Inside the burn barrel, the fire crackled and sparked as if it wanted to soar. Illuminated by the rapidly burning paper, the cherry tree's branches were thrown skyward like a cluster of hostages.

12

A *spark* is a simple, familiar way of describing a spangle of light.

13

The Great White fire, every investigator agreed, could likely have been prevented had those involved paid attention to standard safety practices around the use of pyrotechnics. Less than two years later, a similar pyrotechnic-induced fire destroyed the Republica Cromagnon nightclub in Buenos Aires, Argentina, killing 194 people.

14

A spark from a firework is a particle of red-hot powder ejected from the firework container.

15

Two years before the Manchester, England pop concert disaster, after armed terrorists attacked Le Carillon Bar in France, witnesses said they initially thought firecrackers had gone off before they realized that they were under fire from semi-automatic rifles. "People dropped to the ground. We put a table over our heads to protect us," said a man who was with his wife at the back of the bar. Fifteen people died in the attack on the bar and restaurant, with fifteen severely injured. More than one hundred bullets were fired.

16

Sparks from a sparkler are extremely hot, their temperature anywhere from 1800 degrees Fahrenheit to 3000 degrees Fahrenheit. Last year, in the United States, about 1,200 injuries that were related to sparklers were treated in emergency rooms between June 16 and July 16, what is known as the Fourth of July season. Half of those sparkler injuries happened to children under the age of fourteen.

17

Sparklers leave behind a residue of tiny flecks of burnt iron that is usually not even noticed. Nobody I knew as a boy ever got burned by a sparkler.

18

The most common categories of pyrotechnics are concussion, smoke pot, flame projector, and gerb, which is more complicated and designed to create a jet or fountain of sparks. Various ingredients are added to provide color, smoke, noise or sparks.

19

Ariana Grande, the headliner of the Manchester, England show that was attacked by a suicide bomber, has an enormous fan base among young girls. Video shot inside the venue for that evening's performance showed terrified teenagers screaming as they made their way out amid a sea of pink balloons. Some fans were still wearing the singer and former Nickelodeon TV actress' trademark kitten ears as they fled.

20

By the time my son and I watched the Great White video, we knew that the low ceiling in The Station had been soundproofed with cheap insulation that is not only highly flammable but produces dense, toxic smoke that roiled into the room so thoroughly poisonous those fans had maybe a minute altogether before the odds suggested they were going to die.

21

On a windy, late spring day when I was twelve, I let an open-pit trash fire get away behind the bakery. A couple of burning bags, sparks scattering, tumbled onto the dry, unmown grass. I watched, terrified, as the high grass caught fire and the wind drove the flames toward the bakery. By the time I circled the fire and ran for the back door, the man who lived above the feed store next door scrambled down his back stairs and used a hose he kept for washing his car to extinguish the fire just before it reached the back wall.

22

I ran the Great White video a third time, concentrating on the crowd. A few beer bottles are held aloft in salute to the band. The fans near the front rock in place. The wall behind the band is already on fire, yet a fan in the second row raises a fist in appreciation. One man finally turns toward the camera and gestures toward where the main door must be. Two more patrons turn as the flames reach the roof. And then the camera shuts off, the man doing the filming, I'm sure, heading for the door because it had been noted he was among the survivors.

23

A few months after we watched that video together, before the first time I attended one of his shows in a large arena, my son explained that I should recognize that a bright pinwheel to the side of the stage was a warning that a pyrotechnic concussion was imminent. "Because you're so close to the stage," he said. "So you're ready."

24

On January 27, 2013, at the Kiss nightclub in Santa Maria, Brazil, an accident due to the use of pyrotechnics by the performing live show band caused a fire which resulted in the deaths of at least 236 people, while dozens suffered serious injuries from the fire and smoke inhalation.

25

The 2015 terrorist attack in France was coordinated. More restaurants were fired upon. At Café Bonne Biere and La Casa Nostra pizzeria, five people were killed and eight severely injured. Another occurred at La Belle Equipe bar. "It lasted at least three minutes," one witness said. "Then they got back in their car." Nineteen people died in the shooting, with nine in critical condition. Survivor accounts sometimes included "We thought, at first, we were hearing fireworks."

26

Sparkler bombs are constructed by binding together as many as 300 sparklers with tape, leaving one extended to use as a fuse. Because they don't have a timed fuse, there is some chance they could go off in someone's hand.

27

When I was thirteen, a boy I knew blew his fingers off when he lit a pipe bomb he had finished a few hours earlier. "Isn't this cool?" he'd said the whole time he was setting the fuse. "You should make one." He said he was taking it to a family reunion picnic and placing it in the men's room of the county park. His cousins that were around our age, he said, would be impressed because "It would blow shit up."

28

Children were among the twenty-two people killed in the suicide attack after the Ariana Grande concert. Fifty-nine others were wounded, including some who suffered life-threatening injuries.

29

In large arenas, my son's band performed during intermittent pyrotechnics that erupted near where they were standing. The jets of sparks never reached the high ceilings, all of which were constructed of materials that didn't burn.

30

Once, in the middle of a tour, my son forwarded me a photograph of him standing beside a rock guitarist known as Dimebag Darrell, who had co-founded the well-known heavy metal bands Pantera and Damageplan. Both guitarists are relaxed and smiling after their paths crossed while touring. Shortly after my son sent the photo to me, Dimebag Darrell was shot and killed while performing with Damageplan in a Columbus, Ohio club by a man who jumped on stage.

31

October 30, 2015, at the Colectiv nightclub in Bucharest, Romania, pyrotechnics used by the band Goodbye to Gravity accidentally ignited soundproofing foam on a pillow. The fire quickly spread onto the ceiling and the rest of the club. Sixty-four people died, and more than two hundred were injured. Four members of Goodbye to Gravity lost their lives; only their soloist survived.

32

After I played that Great White video a third time, my son said, "Enough," but I watched once more and focused on the man in the crowd who appeared to be oldest, my age maybe. He is near the back, not bouncing in place. When the film ends, even as some people move past him, he still hasn't turned to rush toward the door.

33

Sparklers burn at temperatures hot enough to melt some metals.

34

Somewhere, I think early every day, the acolyte of terror dreams our bodies as it decides the exact address for delight.

35

The terrorists in France also attacked The Bataclan, a 1500-seat theater located at 50 Boulevard Voltaire in the 11th arrondissement of Paris, where an American band, Eagles of Death Metal, were playing.

Eighty-nine people died as the terrorists fired Kalashnikov-type assault rifles into the crowd. At least ninety-nine others were taken to hospitals in critical condition. "We thought it was fireworks," one survivor said, "but then we realized there were men shooting in all directions. So we all lay on the floor and started crawling toward the stage."

36

Because of a sparkler bomb's construction, whoever is in the vicinity when it is lit will not know the direction in which the explosion will go, or whether the bomb will split and break up. It can explode shrapnel with massive force.

37

After the suicide bomber's attack in England, the security editor for NBC News' U.K. partner ITV News, reported that nuts and bolts were spotted in the arena's foyer, but police, initially, would not comment on whether victims had suffered wounds from shrapnel.

38

One afternoon word came down from the venue that someone had threatened my son's band for that evening's show in a city located hundreds of miles away. We talked on the phone several times while security was being tightened and authorities alerted. I tried to reassure him and myself that it was better to have someone openly declare the threat than keep it a secret because that meant it was highly unlikely that anything would happen that night. "But," my son said, "there's the next show and the next."

TRANSITIONS

A student, once, wrote a story for introductory fiction workshop that ended as a young woman danced slowly with a girl described as beautiful in a shimmering dress that revealed a body that "seemed to be budding as they embraced at the song's last note." The student, two weeks before, had come to class with her head shaved, and now it was thickly stubbled in a way that suggested "manly." She wore a tank top, jeans, and boots. The workshop's eight other young women insisted the story needed "more struggle" because all agreed the beautiful girl was a boy in transition.

While they spoke, I examined the writer's bare, muscular arms and shoulders, the contrast of her soft face to her prickly hair. Mostly, I evaluated how she looked down as if she'd noticed how scuffed her boots were and regretted not polishing them before class. For twenty minutes, as if their mouths were shuttered and locked, none of the six male students spoke. It felt, finally, that they were shaming that student with silence, and I needed to say something positive, but measured, to keep her from screaming. I spoke what amounted to a personal letter, trying to be nuanced about "more struggle," suggesting, at last, to write past the ending, a workshop standby, to see if there might be something more to discover. I allowed the male silence to pass unexamined.

She proofread that draft spotless, but left every detail unchanged. One morning, in December, she came to my office to say she was leaving school after final exams, that she was transferring to a college in another state to live with her friend whose hand she grasped and lifted like a referee. She was euphoric. The young man wore khaki pants and a loose sweater shadowed, but visible underneath his unbuttoned black trench coat. She said, "I want you to meet Candace," and though I offered "Hello, glad to meet you," the young man did not speak, waiting like a beautiful child beside a talkative mother. What came to mind, just then, was "seemed to be budding" and I did not flush with shame.

That was twenty-six years ago, in another century that's vanished in ways beside the passage of time. The young woman was the same age as my daughter who now has two daughters of her own who have posed for prom photos in glittering dresses that flatter their teenage bodies beside boys who are attractive in ordinary ways. Where I still live, an effeminate boy, after being bullied for years, has martyred himself by stepping in front of a speeding truck. There have been vigils on campus in his name. Students holding multi-colored donated candles tell personal stories that are reported in the local newspaper like the ones related during breast cancer month, those histories always accompanied by photographs of survivors or the relatives and friends of those who died after struggles both long and short.

On Exploitation

1

One Saturday afternoon, an email arrived from a woman I hadn't seen in nearly forty years. We'd graduated from college together. She'd married a fraternity brother who lived across the hall from me our senior year. The war in Vietnam separated us within months of graduation. I'd gone to graduate school, in part, to avoid the draft. He'd enlisted in the Air Force, in large part to be trained as a pilot. His roommate was drafted and shipped to Vietnam; mine went to grad school, too.

Someone she knew had stumbled across her husband's name in a poem I'd published. She included the title with her email and added that she "was surprised to see his name" in a poem. I took that to mean she was upset. She'd been a widow, by then, for thirty-six years. The plane he was flying had been shot down in Vietnam.

I wrote back to say I had nothing but good memories of her husband. I apologized and pledged never to be so intrusive again. A good start, but then I added that I'd be happy to send her the book that included that poem, that I'd sign it. When she didn't answer, I began to imagine her sending someone strong and able to beat me silly.

2

During my junior year in college, another fraternity brother I'll call Mike Rogers told me I needed to learn the self-defense of boxing. "With a smart-mouth like yours, somebody's always going to want to kick your ass," he said, and I had to agree.

For sure, I was a trash-talker in basketball, yammering condescending insults at other players. And with a few beers in me, I lapsed into the same sort of snotty talk with strangers who struck me as pretentious or stupid. In short, I was in love with what I saw as cleverness and wit, but Mike Rogers sensed that, though I was eager to abuse people verbally, I was also, in fact, a closet pussy.

We were alone in the recreation room of our fraternity house. He handed me a set of padded gloves. I was taller than Rogers by three inches, but he outweighed me by thirty-five pounds. With those gloves loosely tied on my hands, my arms and shoulders felt as skinny as a twelve-year-olds.

He showed me jabs and hooks, weight-shift and how to bob and weave and keep my arms in and hands high. "Go ahead," he said, "try to hit me. I'll give you a little while before I fight back."

It seemed like an easy lesson, my friend just backing off a step or moving from side to side, gloves up and absorbing all of my half-hearted punches, all of them right-handed. "You have a left hand," he said, pointing out the obvious. I threw another right, discouraged, beginning to prepare a short speech full of promises to practice keeping my mouth shut.

He deflected that punch and said, "You ready to block now?" I nodded, trying to mimic what I'd just seen him do. I didn't even see the first hook. I hadn't thought about anybody using his left hand for anything but jabs and defense.

Rat-a-tat, rat-a-tat, rat-a-tat. The rhythm of his punches against my head came with the sound my old comic book bubbles had used for World War II machine guns. I was suddenly afraid he wouldn't stop until I went down, and then, holding my breath, I covered my face with my forearms and sacrificed every other part of my body.

I was pounded. I was slammed. I was hammered. There was a dog whistle trilling in my head. I took two steps back, and was thrilled when he didn't follow so I could work the gloves loose and let them drop to the floor. "You can't close your eyes like that," he said. "You can't hold your hands like that and expect to live."

I wanted to say something interesting and settled for "Fuck this." The headache he gave me lasted two full days. "Go read some more poems," he said, his way of mocking my English major.

3

Mike Rogers had a point. The seats in my English major literature classes were 90% filled with young women, most of them intending to be public school teachers. None of them, as far as I knew, dreamed of being a college professor or, even better, a full-time writer. I was well on my way to being compulsive about observing and using the lives of everyone around me. The woman who sent the email didn't know that I'd already included her husband in other published work that might soon find its way into magazines, books, and online.

Years earlier, I'd described "Woom! Ball," part of fraternity hazing, in a scene from a coming-of-age story. That time, because it was for "fiction," I'd changed everyone's name, accidentally not compounding her unhappiness with this scene that features her husband, dubbed "Calvin Clifford":

> We circled at three a.m., just before the two-mile run, fifteen pledges who slammed a football broadside into our neighbors' guts. Woom! we hollered, and cupped our hands like running backs to keep ourselves from harm. Woom! Soon there were pledges who moaned. Pledges who doubled up and whined.
>
> Woom! And there were some older brothers who joined, standing among the tough guys like Jim Ulsh and Dave Mazur and Calvin Clifford, the ones who never showed fear or pain. Woom! We fired back, driving that ball into the stomach of seniors just returned drunk from bars. Woom! Until Jim Ulsh took that football point first and came apart inside. Woom! Until Dave Mazur cracked a rib because that football thunked wide of the target area.
>
> We were five days into the mandatory week of no sleep. We were nearly finished with Woom! Ball, one more night, and I was left standing beside Calvin Clifford, who screamed Woom! like a sound could take the air out of me, neither of us knowing he would die in a war that was as small, that night, as our skirmish. Woom! I shouted, and nobody stepped between us until that circle broke for the road where we ran into the town that was sleeping, watching for lights in windows at quarter to four, guessing whether whoever moved there was coming home from trouble or waking into a day that, starting this early, was pain.

4

It was very early in the Vietnam Era when we pledged. Vietnam was a country I couldn't find on a map when I'd entered college. Eventually, I discovered it used to be French Indochina, a country I'd seen described in the set of encyclopedias my mother had bought, one by one, with green stamps and $25 purchases at the grocery store when I was in elementary school.

In 1967, by graduation, being drafted within months was nearly a certainty. For once, I envied fraternity brothers who were cursed with physical problems. One of my best friends, an excellent athlete suddenly limited by a ruined shoulder, received a deferment as a belated consolation prize, but Calvin Clifford went to Vietnam voluntarily. So did a few other frat brothers. Most were simply shipped. The war got worse. I stayed one step ahead of the draft by becoming a high school English teacher like many of those female classmates had done. When my wife and I went to a wedding early in 1969, the fraternity brothers who attended split into two groups—those in uniform and those not. There were nods and handshakes, but mostly the veterans turned their backs and carried on conversations from which male civilians were excluded.

Months later, Calvin ignored me completely at the homecoming football game. He sat with his wife high in the bleachers and apart from my wife and me and a few other couples. He was in full dress uniform. We didn't speak. We didn't even acknowledge each other. Those of us sitting together were the ones who had deferments. Anyone would have figured that out in the fall of 1969. It was the last time I saw him. The last time I saw his wife as well.

5

Calvin's wife had witnessed one of my worst behavior moments. As a senior, depressed and angry and drunk, I shoved my wife-to-be in a way that sent her sprawling off a shoveled sidewalk into the snow of a stranger's front yard. Not a hard shove. Not with malice. More of an impatient push away, but it was undoubtedly a failure of both the heart and the mind. The gesture was indelible, not even now, more than half a century later, erased. To say the snow cushioned her fall would be inexcusable. The snow could have melted that day, and she would have fallen into slush and mud. Its presence was an accident. Less than half a block behind us were Calvin and his soon-to-be-wife.

"She remembers" is what I thought when she contacted me about the poem nearly forty years later. She may or may not have known that Calvin had talked me down later. He'd sat in my room at two a.m. and explained what needed to come next to prevent me from becoming a permanent asshole, advice as valuable as any I've ever received. Chemical imbalance was not an excuse. My second chance needed to be made one-and-done by a lifetime of respect and decency. Through the grace of having more than fifty years to do so, I've managed to work that moment down to something like a smudge.

6

Sometimes, when we played cards, gambling for small stakes to entertain ourselves, Mike Rogers would sandpaper the tattoo of a former girlfriend's name on his shoulder. He may have used that paper on himself in private, too, but shortly before graduation, he was still at it while hands were dealt, the name fainter, but unmistakable. That girl's name accompanied him across the stage as he received his degree.

7

A Master's degree in hand, I landed a new job at a two-year branch campus of Penn State University. In one of my Tuesday-Thursday-Saturday composition classes, I had a student who was a Vietnam veteran. He wrote a stunning essay about being ambushed and surviving while dozens of his comrades were killed. I didn't say a word to him about my draft deferment and self-serving anti-war attitude about Vietnam. I was only a few months older than he was and looked younger. I imagined him sneering at me, someone he must have known would never serve. A coward maybe.

The essay read like fiction, like he was testing me, how naïve or credulous I could be because all I knew about the war was on the six o'clock news. I pointed out a few editing hints and gave him an A, but I didn't write any comments about authenticity, risking nothing but his secret contempt. What I did was attempt to shape my response into a poem.

8

Here is the poem Calvin's widow spoke to in her email. I could have told her that the central event had occurred two years earlier than the date in the title, but she wasn't interested in the nuances of memory or my autobiography or the liberties taken by poets. What mattered was there was no mistaking the presence of her now long-dead husband.

January, 1967: The Impossible

College down to its final semester,
It was, I vowed, my last winter of walking
In terrible weather. The mornings I slogged
Through snow, I thought I could see myself
In the near future of beating the draft,
Shuffling from the physical with the joy
Of a small, but unacceptable flaw.
In Florida, where I planned to be,
Three astronauts had died on the ground,
Inhaling the toxic smoke of a flash fire,
Their deaths grafting them to my classmate
Crushed by a jeep in basic training,
All the danger of the war months away.

That weekend, stopped by sirens, I learned
A girl who'd just said goodbye to me
Had died in the car she'd chosen thirteen miles
Before, that whatever else she'd meant
To say had been hurled through a windshield.
Like she could have been, I was riding
With Calvin Clifford, who was going
To explode in the air over Vietnam,
But right then, just after 2 a.m., we shared
The expletives that follow sudden death
And added the sentences full of "if,"
The paragraphs stuffed with stories meant as
Consolations for the impossible.

On the news, January shutting down,
Were tributes to Grissom, Chaffee, and White
That were still filled with fault speculations
About frayed wires, oxygen level, the hatch
Too difficult to reach, and I told myself
I wanted to hear what that sophomore,
The driver, had to say about speed and ice
And drinking because even I had known
Enough to rely on the judgment
Of Calvin Clifford the way I relied
On somebody every night when what
I wanted was more than two miles from school,
Riding in five cars a week, half of them
Driven by soldiers-to-be, without
Saying a word about the test flights
We were taking to decide what was worth it,
What was not, turning up the radio
So impossibly loud a siren
Couldn't slow any of us who believed
We were learning quickly enough to live.

There was no question which two lines stopped her cold. Even now, with the poem altered by the name-change, the dramatic advantage of those lines is unmistakable. No amount of additional detail in a dozen lines I cut would have provided enough context for those lines to lose their intent. Even if I had included who was driving or where she was sitting next to him in what was commonly called the death seat when the car had struck the bridge, the speed and angle perfectly aligned for ending her life. Even if I had managed to simply not type another word to her after my acknowledgement of guilt.

9

Despite my compromised admission of guilt, I nevertheless wrote about the email exchange incident as well, her husband's name now altered in nonfiction as if that excused me. There would be only a slim chance that she or any of my old fraternity brothers would read what

I'd written without the unlikely indirect help of a Google search of my name. The opening paragraphs, now fifteen years old, are as telltale as Mike Rogers' sandpapered tattoo:

> This morning, as if the past had unwrapped its greasy sack of regret, a woman I haven't seen for more than forty years tells me she's read my poem that uses her dead husband's name, making me expect her curses for describing how we worked as punishment, how, after we swept floors and hauled trash to give us humility we both needed, Calvin Clifford and I, sober on Saturday, were noisy with relief, and yes, pride that we'd finished ten hours for our case of petty, bad behavior.
>
> Because it was February, we'd worked something we called the "light shift," returning our tools in near-dark and standing, for once, among men who worked each weekend at jobs they'd never foreseen as boys, laborers who did what was necessary, the work we wouldn't be repeating, not if we used our brains to earn the future's comfort. Those men huddled inside cars they idled toward warmth, windshields clearing from the bottom in rising moons. From the back of campus, it was sixteen blocks to where our friends were already lively with beer and music, and whether it was the twilight cold or the simple solidarity of work, one car door opened as "Where to?" offer.
>
> The two of us crowded beside that man on a stiff bench seat, the heater full-blast on our feet while Calvin gave directions that stopped that driver early, spilling us into the just-beginning snow two blocks from our Greek-lettered house, standing in front of the cheap apartments where locals lived as if he wanted that maintenance man to believe we were not the spoiled sons of distant fathers. And maybe, because Calvin kept repeating how well we'd cleaned, his bare hands gesturing in the flurries he was already enlisting, his war victim future so close I need his wife not to loathe that poem before I can celebrate our small, unimportant work.

It has taken fourteen years for me to try to fully address that concern.

10

Near the end of my first year of work at the Penn State branch campus, the National Guard shooting happened at Kent State, where I had begun taking classes part-time in order to attain a PhD. The shooting occurred about a hundred yards from where I'd attended a Faulkner seminar. I missed all of it. Minutes before the shooting began, I had boarded a bus that took me to an off-campus parking lot where I retrieved my car for the seventy-five-mile trip home.

The following morning, the academic coordinator I reported to stood outside of his office as if he'd been expecting me to pass by. "So," he said, "it finally happened."

Though there was no question what he meant, I said, "What's that?"

"The protestors. Some of them got what was coming to them."

I fingered the keys in my pocket like a blind man choosing the one that would make the best weapon. "They were murdered," I said.

"Really?" he said. "What about the shots that were fired first at the National Guard?"

"That didn't happen."

"But you'd have to admit there's another side of this story, wouldn't you? I'm sure you'd agree there are a great many contradictions?"

"The killers are lying."

He turned away. He paused and looked back as if he'd forgotten something. The campus didn't close. My composition students struggled with argument and persuasion. Not one of them in the three sections I taught wrote about the Kent State shootings.

A week later, the academic coordinator walked into my office to say, "Those pictures of the dead students they had in *Life* are all from high school. Everybody knows they didn't look like that when the Guard fired."

11

Rich Cook (another now-altered name) was in the National Guard. A few weeks later, he and Mike Rogers were among a half dozen old fraternity brothers at a house party I attended near Youngstown. Rich Cook had lived next door to Rogers, just across the hall during my sophomore year. His car, that year, had been immersed in a flash flood near his home, and the stink refused to leave throughout an entire semester. A telephone had hung on the wall between his door and Rogers'. Three times that year Cook had torn loose the black receiver and carried it into my room after two a.m., each time silhouetted against the hall light, spitting, "It's for you" as if that joke could never grow old.

Since finishing my third beer, I'd been using my near-miss with eye-witnessed history to condemn President Nixon, Ohio's Governor Rhodes, and each and every one of the Kent State shooters. Cook, though he was avoiding the draft by being in the Guard, was soon drunk and angry and ready, he said, to shoot me if history repeated itself. He said he had a pistol in that long-ago flooded Ford I could see through the screen door where white moths were frantic to enter, and he wondered out loud if I'd piss myself if he decided to show-and-tell me just how cowardly I could be up close with him and Rogers and Bob Bowers, a fraternity brother who was just back from two tours with a pair of Purple Hearts, somebody who'd survived Hamburger Hill and nameless night patrols.

Cook asked if I was a Communist now or just some big-mouth asshole drinking free beer with someone like Bowers who had proved he was worth a shit. Rogers said nothing, but he looked like he remembered my acquiescence to his padded fists, and now Bowers was so tight-lipped I was ready to renounce my years of second-hand graduate school essays, all of those sweet-sounding platitudes seeming as simple as pre-meal prayers while I composed apologies and expected him to lay a combat-tested beating upon me.

I could say the overhead kitchen light beamed a Saint Paul moment of self-knowledge and conversion, but what it did was flicker once when the refrigerator hummed into life just before Bowers said, "Fuck the Guard" so matter-of-factly I heard the period drop into place, ambushing one argument, at least, in Youngstown where August was fishtailing into September.

12

When school began in September, the Penn State Beaver Campus faculty fielded a team in the intramural seven-on-seven touch football league. One of us had played major college football at West Virginia; the rest of us boasted some high school memories or gym class heroics, good enough, it turned out, to go 5-1, tied for first and paired against a team of guys who all wore the same high school varsity jacket to our late October playoff game. Five of them were enrolled in one of my sections of introductory composition, two of them carrying Ds, another an F, but it wasn't their grades that made them see me as the enemy, it was my status as the Kent State radical because I'd spoken briefly at a campus rally and submitted a "Kent State was Murder" opinion piece to the campus newspaper.

They parked their cars together in the commuter lot, and every one of them sported bumper stickers that read *America—Love It or Leave It.* As if there were a dress code, all of them wore their hair short, and none of them had sideburns like I did. Three of them had made a point to tell me they had older brothers in Vietnam.

I wasn't thinking about any of that until I went out for a pass, the WVU alum tossing a perfect spiral my way. Just as I extended for the ball, the world suddenly spun out of control. I lay on my back for a few seconds to get reoriented. "What happened?" I asked when I got back to the huddle.

"You were clotheslined," the former Division I player said, laughing as if he'd enjoyed the incompletion.

Clotheslining in touch football seemed like an obvious penalty, but the student referee standing nearby was expressionless, his whistle quiet. I didn't even know which of the players on the other team had thrown his forearm under my chin and spun me head over heels.

A few plays after that, my legs back under me, I caught a short, sideline pass and turned up field, taking one step before I took a shoulder and forearm in the chest. I fumbled, but the ball tumbled out of bounds. I sank to one knee and tried to get my breath, waiting for the penalty to be assessed. "Good hit," somebody said. Nothing was called.

I understood I was getting my teacher evaluation. Like Mike Rogers and Rich Cook, those students thought they knew me for a coward. Four weeks later, Calvin Clifford was killed in Vietnam.

13

Vietnam was still more than a year away for Calvin Clifford and his roommate when, not long before graduation, my roommate and I joined them for a weekend at a deserted farmhouse owned by a relative of Calvin's roommate. We weren't there for late-college binge drinking; our girlfriends came along. No one had lived in the house for a couple of years. We walked around what was left of the farm's fields, played touch football, slow-drank beer or wine, and ate hot dogs we jammed onto pointed sticks to cook over a fire. After dark, we moved into separate rooms for the night, devising beds from abandoned furniture and sleeping bags. It felt daring and sexy, but before long we understood there were rats or mice or both in large numbers, and they had sensed every crumb we hadn't picked up.

Some of us chose to sit up for the night; some of us chose to sleep outside. No one lay back down inside the house of scurrying paws. In an annual succession, three of the couples were soon married—Calvin that summer, me the next, and then my roommate the next. Despite the rats and approaching final exams, the weekend felt bucolic. Consequently, those two days never demanded to be on the page until now. Throughout a half century of opportunity, my choices, when writing about Calvin and the other fraternity brothers I lived with for three years, have all been grounded in their proximity to violence.

14

The note Calvin's widow sent seemed to have a tone of repressed violence. I've taken her subsequent fifteen years of silence as confirmation. If I could convince her to listen to me at all, it would be to say how Calvin had, in some significant ways, saved my life from careening off in another direction that would, without question, have been worse. Though she might, with good reason, answer by reminding me how his unselfishness had gone unrewarded while a prick who writes poems and stories and essays has lived to take advantage of the dead.

15

The war staggered on, but my deferment advantage survived. A few years after the shootings, while I was writing my dissertation, I became old enough to store my draft card in a drawer as a souvenir. I was still teaching at the Penn State branch campus, still manning three thirty-five-students-per-class of Introductory Composition. After a few months, not one of those students asked about the National Guard. What's more, not one ever mentioned it in the thousands of essays I read before I left for another position.

One morning, the local newspaper carried a story about a son killing his father in self-defense. The father ran a karate school in a town near the campus. He was a certified and much-decorated expert, and he had seen to it that his son was an expert as well. When their argument went out of control, they'd fought, using all of their karate skills, and the son, the student who'd written that extraordinary war experience essay during my first term, had finally strangled his father with nunchucks because, he explained, "My father would have done the same to me."

I reread the story as if I could discover something I'd missed about what sort of disagreement would lead to a father and son fighting hand-to-hand to the death. According to the story, they'd battled for nearly an hour because their mastery of self-defense was so evenly matched. At once, I knew it was a story I would use.

By then I had a wife, an infant son, and a small house that was surrounded by nothing more than rhododendron bushes. For a few moments, I sat in the safety and quiet of a newspaper and a cup of coffee while considering which details could seed a story or a poem. And now, after forty-eight years, whether with selfishness or gratitude, I need my dead friend's widow to know that I walked to where my wife and small child were sleeping and listened to them breathing.

The Habits of Eating

The Ignition Point of Paper

The first evening of war, half an hour after a fireman snatched our dinner from the oven to fling outside, my wife and I watched a map of the Middle East as if it were animated, the reporters doing voice-overs from countries certain to suffer. We listened to faraway air raid sirens. We heard sentences built around warhead, payload, and missile range. I wondered out loud about which of those reporters might be self-consciously slow putting on a gas mask, what symptoms of poisoning might be visible. My wife said nobody would hesitate, not when they expected the alternative was paralysis or death. We started rethinking dinner, what else to eat with war because chicken-in-a sack lay charred and sprawled in our front yard.

We settled on frozen pizza. The boxes had directions that called for preheating to 425 degrees. The oven was still vaguely warm. An hour earlier, when I'd opened the oven door, the paper bag had flared. When I closed it, I could watch the cyanotic smolder of it through the glass. I said *451*, remembering, from school, a novel about books burned by firemen, the classics consumed by flames 49 degrees below the heat our recipe had suggested for baking. I'd felt like a science text, like bagging my own bookish body for the torch. On television, the President stared and told us, "This is no Vietnam," sounding like the President who told us, "We'll nail the coonskin to the wall" the year I learned the ignition point of paper, and I left the gospels of the president to resack that sorry chicken, add it to our week's curbside bags. Though by daylight something had shredded its way inside and scattered the carcass on the snow, none of it retrieved by the garbage man who refused, by contract, to accept anything not bagged and tied.

Inedia

A few years earlier, when we'd moved, we'd discovered that a nearby village had been suffering from an underground mine fire for twenty years. Centralia, by then, was being emptied because of subsidence, the threat of carbon monoxide, and what was proving to be the hopelessness of extinguishing the fire. Some expert declared there was enough coal remaining in the seams to burn for 200 years. The main highway through the town began to crack, smoke escaping through the fissures.

Near where we'd lived before was a neighborhood grown infamous for having slime bubble up through its stricken lawns. Decades earlier, Hooker Chemical had dumped 21,800 tons of hazardous waste into the abandoned Love Canal, covered it up, laid down some top soil, and sold the land to developers. By the time we lived in Western New York, families were being shuttled from the Love Canal site because of miscarriages, the threat of cancer and other possible environmentally-related diseases. Residents of both neighborhoods talked in similar ways about the hammerlock of property, the eye gouge of ownership. In one parable of industry was the blasphemy of coal barons; in the other was the heresy of the landfill. Such a sampler of sadness, I told my wife, it's like we can press our disasters like chocolates, using our fingers to find cherries or butter creams or caramels. And when there was a sweet story of a boy in Centralia being saved by tree roots after tumbling down a hole created by the mine fire, it seemed more miraculous than the survival of the woman who, recently found, had lived two weeks without eating, the miracle explained by an expert who told us she crash-dieted before her voyage to shipwreck. She'd grown used to little food, a sort of cross-training for starvation, and I recalled the Woman of Norwich, who lived for twenty years without eating, according to Francis Bacon, who might be Shakespeare, according to someone else.

The Maggot Farmer

That summer, maggots swarmed in our garbage when the bags came time to be carried to the curb. I made lifting my son's job, told him they were only larvae, what we could use for bait to hook barble and bream. I talked and talked about what I'd read but didn't know. I mentioned the farmer who had once shown me the carcasses of cattle he stored behind his house. "For coarse fishermen," he had explained while I stared and retreated. I told my son that Aristotle claimed maggots were conceived by rotten meat, how he thought he saw insects birthed by mud. How he wrote it down and landed on a list of fools in a book I showed my son, one notch below Bill Pickering, the astronomer who said, in the twentieth century, the spots on the moon are huge swarms of insects. Maybe, I said, he let his garbage grow wings instead of flushing his cans with disinfectant. Maybe NASA filmed the astronauts in Nevada like the skeptics claimed because they feared the lunar surface writhed with grubs. And though my son insisted no one grows maggots for a living, twice that summer we dropped worms into fouled creeks for sport. We examined the teeth we found while digging for bait, thinking, if we studied forensics, we might claim discoveries others would believe for as long as it takes to turn up something to disprove them.

The Habits of Eating

Rabies. Bubonic Plague. AIDS. Botulism. I study a list of the deadliest illnesses, including kuru, the laughing sickness, a sure death that comes from eating the raw brains of the dead, gulping them, after battles, to absorb the prowess of the defeated warriors. How stupid, we're likely to scoff, or so absurdly vain, yet we're often stubborn, fierce with ethnic excuses for the animals we devour: snakes, dogs, beetles, ants. Or balot, the Tagolog name for one more improbable, long-lived recipe:

> First, be patient. Wait the number of days it takes to hatch a duck, and then snatch that egg, hard-boil that fetus, and eat the unborn whole—feathers, bill and bones.

Like veal, you might say, or lamb, speaking like an illustrator of books for babies who want smiles in their barnyards, ear-to-ear grins on Flopsy, Mopsy and Topsy. And probably you've owned a few of those living toys, and all of them have died like a series of hamsters who quiver with metabolism so rapid they flare and go out like filaments. So we float and grow, transform from the curled worm common to us all: Flippers to feet, tails retracted, the brain's circuitry connected, and, if not spoiled, set loose by those who could eat us.

Don't Let the Moon Break Your Heart

Unable to sleep one night, I carried a bag of potato chips downstairs and watched a three-a.m. B-movie, an early Sixties dubbed-in saga about Spaniards reaching the New World. The Cortez lookalike stepped ashore saying, "That's one small step for man," so he might, in first run, have moved Neil Armstrong to tears. Or all along, those astronauts, sworn to secrecy in Nevada, were prepped for bogus landings with lines penned for beefcake stars. David Scott. James Irwin. John Young. By then I needed an almanac to name the moonwalkers, sleeplessness enough to discover crib-sheet dialogue in an old Conquistadore film.

It wasn't the only time. My first full-time job was teaching English to the teenage children of fathers who mostly worked at Valvoline, the railroad yards, and Armco. Arriving early most days, I let the night-shift janitor say the moon just conquered lay fifty miles outside Las Vegas, that close, as he showed me a book that proved the earth flat, pointed out stars that clustered where heaven lay. I drank coffee and ate custard doughnuts while he explained the hierarchy of halo shapes, the maintenance for wings. Some nights, he said, you can see shipments of the saved arriving in light—The Pearly Gates, could I see their shape? And I stared, two hours before I had to say a word, mouthing to myself "Don't Let the Stars Get in Your Eyes," singing like an armored extra in a foreign musical who's lip-synced, later, to show his hands flew apart for balance, not joy, before he tumbled off the delicate wafer of the just-claimed land.

The Mayan Syndrome

Throughout the summer after that brief war, my children claimed we were the only family they knew that ate dinner together. What's more, we were the only family that ate "real meals" while their friends ate pizza, hot dogs, tacos and instant mac 'n cheese. The news began to warn that parts of our planet were missing. Soil presumed drowned. Ozone kidnapped and murdered. If we weren't careful, we could expect a pandemic of environmental disasters. As if it were a supplement to those stories, a feature on the Mayan Syndrome, the mystery of that culture's inexplicable loss, appeared in a magazine I subscribed to. Now even the ruins were being abused. The man in a photograph was sweeping his patio built from temple blocks, feeding his pigs from an artifact altar. Nothing prospers, the man claimed. Rain has moved elsewhere, the solution of sea-turtle sacrifice to the rain god Chac proved false. These swine need to eat, he said, and I could have smirked and imagined that when their trough catches the sun at exactly the proper angle, the pigs paused to think of miracles, but I had planted stones of my own, spreading them from my sliding door in the sign used for calculating square root. It might have passed for a symbol, the spread stones meant to be read from the heavens to keep evil from my doorstep, pass it along to my neighbors, their daughter disappeared and likely dead, who weren't, in those drought months, pleading for rain when they faced their altar. She won't be dead, not to us, they said, until her body is found. Like MIA's. Like the charity bracelet names. Corporal Connors, I read from the one in my basement drawer, but he was still missing somewhere in a Vietnam rain forest, immortal almost, like the souls of Mayans, like ozone and soil and the woman who may be buried near our neighborhood like one of those bodies cleverly hidden in the eye-teasers printed in a book of puzzles.

The Autonomic Curse

Mac Norton, the Human Aquarium, claimed to possess the multiple stomachs of a cow, swallowing six goldfish, twelve frogs, and delivering all eighteen, one at a time, between his lips. Never lost a prop, he said, resurrecting them in minutes, but there were frogs, once, in Australia, who laid eggs and ate them, waiting out hatching and the transformational nursery weeks until, one by one, fully formed, those children spit themselves out like one more evolution wonder. Nothing like my friend's cyanotic son, his head huge and hopeless in the pictures he handed me, once, like a deck of cards. Another week, maybe two, he quoted his doctor, though I didn't see even that chance in any of the photos from the thirty-six hours of breathing. And those odd Australian frogs? They are extinct.

Remedies

Before school began I needed to drive my daughter ninety miles to a television studio to be interviewed for what proved to be thirty seconds of air time. The day before, in court, a convicted killer had claimed he was a holy assassin because God had asked him to murder. I am a remedy, he said like a junta, and on the way home, while we were stuck in a flagman's traffic beside a mile-long graveyard for cars, I decided to get off at the next exit and search for the murder site. My daughter guessed half a million rusted bodies were taking the cure, enough, maybe, to be Guiness World Records famous, and I answered by wheezing like an ad opener for the inhalant I was determined not to use. The road crew slouched on shovels while I remembered the list-book lines on Salisbury, the man who became a food when he convinced people to eat, well done, ground beef three times a day. "With hot water," he added, menu for the end of asthma, "with reasonable habits."

Lately I'd been unreasonable, weaning myself from a thousand milligrams per day of Theolair and waking inside the mathematics of asthmatic strangling. So far, I'd survived, walking breath back into myself, researching holistic remedies for health. In Ethiopia, for instance, one emperor ate the Bible to restore himself—Psalms for discomfort, Exodus for disease. He sent Zachariah, not hamburger, to his bronchi; he swallowed Genesis instead of apricot pits or brain waves, choosing from his personal list of *lubberwort,* one word I'd taught Shannon, explaining her diet, the valueless foods that make us stupid, her soda and puffed cheese and cookies. She'd just been sick enough to require prescription tubes; she'd recovered and returned to *lubberwort,* and when we finally escaped construction, we entered the killer's neighborhood, the six hundred block of mayhem where we parked and half recalled the shape of the death-house tree behind the TV newsman. My daughter stood in front of four likely trunks until I caught the curve of a branch, the black fork jutting exactly the way God's gunman must have seen it before slipping inside, and she posed there, fist to her mouth like a microphone, ready to speak to the air.

The Air of Delicate Pastry

Francis Battalia, years ago, ate stones by the spoonful, chased them with beer and shook the sack of his stomach for evidence. After his feats became popular, stone eaters flourished. The thinnest drank water to flush their gravel, fueled one cult of reduced calories, early converts to the slow furnace of zoologists who extend the lives of test mice, these days, by diminishing their charted dinners. In our country of sad diets, we choose the stones of low sugar, low sodium, the rocks of low fat and cholesterol. We suck and roll them back our tongues to gulp doses for the fears that keep us cautious. Which bite brings the AIDS of the arteries or the stiff botulism of the heart? Though he made them, my father wouldn't eat the fat ladylocks and thick whoopee pies, refusing their sweet, white sculptures of crème. Lard and sugar, he told me. A little water. Fool's food, he said, like the cornstarch of bargain pies, the refined sweeteners of icing he tasted, judged, and spit out while he slathered it for millworkers, baking from midnight till morning, stopping with doughnuts turning gold in the deep-fat fryer. He ate wheat bread, the rich custard of éclairs. He explained fiber and eggs and the legitimate sugars of fruit. He praised the natural holes in bread, none of them like the homogenized air of Wonder loaves, their dough a miracle of emulsifiers, whipped and balanced like flavored scoops of soft ice cream, perfect squares of processed cheese. And then he described the air of delicate pastry, how it lightens the richness of butter, how he folded and sheeted, folded and sheeted until that sweet dough spread so fine and light it released the breeze of desire, the breath of gratitude, what works to support us, the air from which we never grow estranged.

The Hot Wings Wager

Once, during the time we lived near Love Canal, I took the dare of a bar that promised gift certificates for downing a double order of "Diablo wings" in fifteen minutes. They triggered tears, revved the wheeze and cough of reflex with jalapeno and japones, guero and tepin, and the chiles unnamed and mythical as holy mushrooms. I was ready to spend my winnings on beer and shrimp, authentic blues in an uptown bar. "Hot cherry," I said. "Cayenne." I recited my picante vita, claiming fifteen minutes of pain so tiny I'd laugh, later, at apprehension. And I thought of my father, who believed in the green pepper and the green pepper only. Who swore food on the table showed a man for who he is, one reason he sometimes wished for the selfish to choke, the rich to aspirate, hurrying themselves to hell. Like this, I thought, swallowing fire like a flame eater, bolting eight, frantic to finish and recognizing, more clearly than ever, the scald of stupid choice. Ten. Twelve. Halfway to paradise, the cook explained—something like sex, like the multiplications of filth. Sixteen and stalled. Eighteen and the betrayal of the esophagus and stomach, the giveback of foolishness to the visible word. Though even after vomit, after the violence of the body's refusal, I was regretting its checks and balances, how we're limited by the sober sonata of involuntary sense.

Now You Know

One Saturday morning when I was twelve, my father offered me a choice between a calf's brain or kidneys that he'd bought fresh for frying. The brain was impossible and refusing both was an option guaranteeing ridicule, so I asked what a kidney tasted like. "Better than you think," he said. "You'll know it's ready when the stink goes away." Slathered with salt, the kidney was so rich with fat I loved it. "See there," my father said, "now you know." The grease pooled around my scrambled eggs and the rich rye bread I used to sop it up, bread he'd baked hours before, on his feet all night, anticipating those meals of organs, teaching the body.

China, 2001

After our children left home, after my wife and I had stopped eating red meat, followed by her abandoning chicken as well, I visited China with students and other faculty from the university where I work. The third day we rode a bus north from Beijing through neighborhoods that seemed closer to the year 1001 than 2001. Because a group I'd never heard of until, shortly before our trip, they were on the news for destroying ancient Buddhist and Hindu artifacts, I asked a colleague who teaches political science to explain who the Taliban were. Awful, she said, far worse than the Communists for the people of Afghanistan.

Everything seen as sacred by anyone other than them represents a false god, she added, accounting for why the world's tallest standing Buddha had been destroyed a few weeks earlier.

That evening, when the students we accompanied whined about eating nothing but local everywhere we traveled, I vowed to try everything that was served. The next day, at our northernmost location near the Gobi Desert, the students were even pickier, skipping half the choices. I worked fatty boiled meat around my mouth and swallowed; I tried something yellow that was cooked but had the consistency of wood. Finally, I stuffed something into my mouth I couldn't swallow. I chewed and chewed as the students prattled on about how primitive everything was, the bathrooms in particular. I chewed some more and surrendered, spitting the congealed mess into a napkin. My Chinese colleague, who was leading the tour, laughed and said, "Duck's feet, very difficult."

After The Daily Show

Two years later, one of my students traveled to Centralia to research an essay. She interviewed the mayor, a man recently the object of a mocking, false interview on *The Daily Show*. He was in his eighties and had twelve constituents left to govern. "His wife served me lemonade and cookies," she said. "They were the nicest people." Her descriptions drew me to drive there again, walking where hundreds of houses once stood before hiking to where the trees were still green to stand among them a few feet from where the forest was skeletal. "It made me angry," she said, "to see all the tourists taking photographs."

Love Canal, by then, had been declared clean and taken off the Superfund list. What's more, though one group of houses had been razed, 260 others had been refurbished and sold to families at 20% below value to repopulate the area. Occidental Petroleum had purchased the land and contained the pollution. They'd renamed the housing development Black Creek Village and welcomed the new homeowners. "This is a victory," a spokesperson for the Environmental Protection Agency declared.

At my university, students had placed tiny flags in front of the campus center, one for every soldier killed in the Middle East. Each week they added new flags, the display growing like an enormous, spreading rash.

The Long Line for Brains

Three more years passed. In a town I visited, the longest line at any of the booths at its annual fair led to brain sandwiches. "Pigs' brains this year," my guide said, "because mad cow scares off the customers." She was twenty-one, showing me and my wife an hour of southern Indiana before I was supposed to read and discuss my poems and stories about Pittsburgh, where I'd eaten liver and hearts, stomach and kidneys. "It's a week's worth of cholesterol on a bun," she said, as if that was more frightening than the remoteness of mad cow disease. And yet there was a whole-wheat option and a short list of condiments, including onions. "They're the best," she said, laughing. That afternoon, loitering among a hundred Hoosiers swallowing something like a heart attack, I thought of my father's heart at nearly ninety despite dozens of Saturday breakfasts, not only of brains, but also of chicken livers and gizzards and hearts, all of them fried crisp in grease.

How to Enjoy High Meat

High meat is raw and fermented, the blood becoming like alcohol. For beginners, marble-sized bites are recommended, bolting them down without chewing and quickly, too, as insurance against the stink. There's extra energy you will gain, so much of it you should avoid eating at night for fear of sleeplessness. One dieter says he began with buffalo liver, eight pounds of it he nibbled for a week. And once, a month-old deer brain because he loved organ meat. As for any diet, there are some issues. Fish turns peppery and acrid. Scallops and sea bass have limits of four or five bites a day. Beef pancreas so quickly turns gooey and flavorless, it's nearly impossible to tolerate at all.

Subsidence

One night, after we'd driven fifteen miles in order to eat at a restaurant for which he had a coupon that said, "Buy one meal and get one of equal or lesser value for free," my father had me drive through the new housing plan less than a mile from his house. Two streets featured strings of sawhorses with flashing lights. "Subsidence," he said. "They built over the old mines even though everybody knew." One of those streets was closed to traffic. "Three houses here are abandoned," he said. More will surely go."

Eating the Brains

When he sees calves' brain on the appetizer menu, my son, forty years old now, insists we order a plate. He's heard my brain stories more than once; he's testing me. When they arrive, they're soft, nearly mushy, a consistency that somehow surprises. The flavor isn't as distinctive as I expect. It is closer to bland than any other organ meat I've tried. When we finish, both of us are triumphant but disappointed that finishing the brain didn't announce itself as some sort of rare achievement. Veterans of organ food, we ask ourselves "What's left?" and imagine intestines, lungs, and, at last, testicles.

Artifacts

Now there are fewer than ten people left living in Centralia. The government waits them out. When everyone is dead, the site will be deserted except for tourists who come to marvel at the ground's heat, the dead forest, and the emptiness.

Now there are reports that the new residents of Love Canal are falling ill and having miscarriages. Lawsuits have been filed; a thousand more have been threatened. Denials proliferate.

When I see photographs of 3000-year-old Assyrian artifacts being destroyed in Syria by ISIS, I think of walking across campus to the office of the political science professor, but the destruction feels so familiar I don't know what else I could ask her. Instead I open a breakfast bar and watch a video of men with their faces covered pounding on the downed statues with sledge hammers until they seem little more than gravel.

This Week

For my son's birthday, we go to a restaurant that specializes in chicken wings. His son, lately turned teenager, is with us. There are dozens of sauces to choose from, an elaborate chart that is scaled to the peppers' heat, but one at a time, we all order the standard "medium." Both mine and my grandson's wings are boneless, so we eat them with a knife and fork. My son gives up before he finishes, saying his are too spicy. I help my grandson finish his. On the television news, there is a mention of a single local casualty in the Middle East, someone killed on his third tour. "That war," I say to my grandson, "is as old as you are," but he is distracted because every other large screen is tuned to baseball, basketball, softball, soccer, and hockey. My son wants to talk about the memoir I've published, the terrible food I was forced to eat and the odd behavior of my parents, mixing those items as if they're connected by some strange cause and effect. Though I have included specific details about their reliance on recipes and prejudices passed down from their parents like faulty chromosomes, I begin to defend them, starting with "Despite all that …"

Telephone

1

I ask my wife if she remembers who, using a specially-designed extension handle, repainted our dining room's cathedral ceiling. "Of course, I do," she says. "He was disgusting. A week later, he called and said he wanted to rape me." As soon as I hesitate to speak, she stares. After I admit I've forgotten that call, she glares.

2

Late in the 1950s, my family's dial phone was heavy and black and sat on a narrow counter just wide enough to hold it between the refrigerator and the electric stove. It was on a party line with other phones—sometimes, when I picked it up, I could hear other people talking. It was thrilling and then it was scary when some stranger would say get off the line whoever you are often punctuated with blasphemies I had been warned never to say because god would overhear and punish me. And sometimes, especially men, they used words that were obscenities, rough and threatening, but carrying my parents' wrath rather than god's.

I never called anyone until I was eight or nine, and then only with permission. My mother, when those calls became more frequent, cautioned, "Watch your mouth; you never know who's listening," citing a trilogy of gossip, government, or God. For a year or two, I did, but only because I didn't yet know the obscenities and none of my calls were like the ones I regularly listened to, most of them women who spoke in stories of complaint and scandal.

What was required of me was silence, even when a woman would say, "Who's there?" or some obscenity from the thesaurus for forbidden phrases. Mostly, they watched their mouths, but some afternoons their voices lowered to tell tales stuffed with polio, leukemia, and deaths by accidents that had missed me for so long I thought of myself, by eleven, as immune. More often, they fed me chemotherapy and catheter, excision and metastasis, words I researched in a dictionary I used during calls, during sixth grade, I made to Nancy Harter, all of them undetected by my mother because they were local, Nancy's house within a radius tighter than the destruction zone of a hydrogen bomb.

Fellatio, Nancy said one afternoon, not watching her mouth, then cunnilingus, repeating the proper words for pleasures she had discovered in a dictionary of her own, researching how variations of joy could be brought to the vagina and the penis, both of us not knowing who might be listening. We were excited to expose our mouths, speaking with an untested authority, as if we knew the future of our intimacy, as if our lives were larger through language that named the body's curiosities. After she read the definitions of a new word we were both silent for a few seconds, something like the false endings in songs we loved for a few weeks, a space we seemed to be filling in with expectations before we said the crude words for those acts out loud, learning to translate. What made it more thrilling was imagining that someone was listening.

3

My wife doesn't wait for me to ask how she could identify him. "He tried to disguise it by deepening it and sounding hoarse, but I recognized his voice," she says. "He had just been inside our house. I can quote him exactly: 'Lock your doors because I'm coming to rape you.'" She pauses as if I need to insert an apology, but I have nothing but silence. When she begins again, her voice has risen. "Absolutely, I'm sure about that one. And I had to see him a few more times. At the post office. In the grocery store. It made me sick every time."

4

The morning my daughter was born, my wife, hours from delivery, answered a call that came so early, the late September morning still suppressed by fog, it sounded like emergency until a man's hoarse voice whispered how hard he was thinking about her soft, fuckable body before he lapsed into nothing but heavy breathing. Over forty years now, our rotary phone an antique, my daughter with girls of her own, but right then, between contractions, my wife said, "I think I recognized him," naming a man who worked for her, somebody she had hired.

"Impossible," I said, citing how swollen she must have been the last time they had met, spinning suspicion into accident and driving slowly without mentioning our neighbor, even the day before, watching her cross our just-mown lawn from what I knew was his bedroom window, or how I'd noticed that habit of his for months, often pleased he surely coveted his neighbor's wife. I might as well have called her myself to heavy-breathe I needed men to desire her. And yes, this morning, a man I know boasted how fuckable his daughter had become, then laughed as if confident I'd agree, as if he carried private photographs to share with someone who might confess to calling a woman he knew to covet her with words, excusing himself with self-disgust and rage, trusting such a weak, perpetual penance substitutes for decency day-to-day.

5

My wife's rage, she says, is ongoing. She thinks about it without the sort of prompting I've just given her. That man she was so sure had called has been dead for more than ten years. Whatever punishment she wished upon him is impossible. There is an accusation in her voice, and I have no alibi to put distance between me and shame. I have as much chance of being exonerated as I do of successfully calling the dead to deliver a promise to add punishment to that caller's personal hell.

6

Decades ago, when my younger son was in sixth grade, a policeman called to let me know someone in a town twenty-five miles away had accused my son of making obscene phone calls. "I thought I should let you know and you could handle this before I have to," the policeman said. "Mr. Beaver says it's your boy. He has him on his answering machine. We need you to come in and listen to the tape. Bring your boy, let him listen to himself."

"I don't understand," I said, the sticky film of embarrassment adhering to the entire length of my body. "How does he know it's my son?"

"He leaves his name each time. He tells Mr. Beaver who he is."

I was relieved. "Nobody does that," I said.

"You'll be shocked. I guarantee it. He left his phone number, too. It's a plea for help. Wait till you hear these."

"It's a friend," I said. "It's somebody my son knows trying to be funny."

"Nobody's friend talks like this," he said, and I allowed silence to extend, waiting for common sense to arrive, but "Bring your boy in. You'll see who's mistaken," ended that call.

When I relayed the message to my son, he was expressionless. "You can check," he said. "That guy lives so far away, those calls would be on our phone bill."

"So, there it is," I said. I had a detective for a son.

A few days later, the policeman called back. "You haven't brought your boy in," he said.

"That's right. My phone bill doesn't have a single call to the town where Beaver lives."

"That proves nothing," the policeman said, but he never called again, and soon the incident became a joke among me and my two sons, one of us saying, "Beaver called" to laughter.

7

I remember that house painter—his thick muscular arms, his protruding belly, how the word squat comes to mind when I describe him to myself. He was twenty-five years older than we were, recently retired. Not, in my imagination, a poster-body for rapist or even a man who fantasizes rape. He was, give or take, the same age I am now.

8

Five years after my son's bout with Mr. Beaver, I received an obscene call of my own, a man's voice repeating the ways he wanted to please one private part of my body, his breath and moans building to a sudden cry that ended in a line gone dead.

Fifteen years before we had Caller ID, I was left to wonder who had confessed such desire. For weeks, each man I knew became a suspect. I listened for the caller's inflections, the clues of his final vowels. I imagined how many times he'd considered calling before that night, whether he knew my wife was at a meeting or it was luck enhanced by persistence. Most often, I wondered whether he'd called before and hung up when she'd answered, that she kept his multiple queries secret because she had deduced their reason.

Regardless, that voice never again found me alone, so much time passing I had to accept it was random, that any man who answered would do, that the caller preferred me to be, not who I was, but what he imagined, someone in love with being wanted, eager maybe, pleased to be objectified, even targeted, as far as I could extend that sentence without self-incrimination.

Though, for months, I left the phone unanswered when I was alone, allowing each caller to leave a message, yet listening for an extended silence that might be longing to hear my triggering voice.

9

From our balcony, the house painter would have looked down at my wife going through the movements of an ordinary late afternoon and early evening. He would have been able to stare, the track lights on the wall below the balcony railing brightly illuminating her body as she passed beneath him. His gaze would have had time to cover every intimate area of her body each time he paused while perfecting the paint on our difficult-to-reach ceiling, leaving not a spot or a corner untouched by the well-practiced, efficient extension of his arms.

Missing

First, a one-day record for local snowfall. By the second day, fifty-two inches had accumulated, the region's roads impassable. The weather grew colder, ice thickening on the nearby river. Then, a warm spell. Finally, heavy, late January rain. Serious flooding predicted.

Early Saturday morning, the world still dark outside, I was revising a story in my university office when I noticed a strange light reflected on the computer screen. When I turned, I saw that the floor was flooding, the overhead lights mirrored on the shallow pool of water expanding across the thin carpet. For now, the puddle wasn't threatening my books or furniture. I had half an hour of what I believed was important work to complete before I had to move things and call maintenance.

A few minutes later, the door to the building in which my office was housed swung open. Maintenance reading my mind, I said to myself, but almost immediately, a state trooper appeared in my open doorway. I could think of no other reason for him personally tracking me down than one of my three children, all of whom, ages eighteen, twenty-one, and twenty-four, lived elsewhere, was severely injured or dead. In a word, I was terrified. "I understand you know Lawrence Abrams?" the policeman said.

It's not my kids, I thought, and answered, "Yes."

"Are you, by any chance, aware of where he may have spent the night?"

A recently retired colleague, Larry Abrams was a friend who lived in a small house in a frequently flooded riverbank area. "No," I said.

"He's missing," the policeman said. "His car was discovered unattended this morning not far from his home. We're in the process of contacting friends and former co-workers, those with whom he may have found shelter."

By now, missing seemed a synonym for dead. Hovering between relief and sorrow, I waited for the state trooper to decide how to end the interview.

"We don't know, for certain, whether he has been harmed," the policeman said.

"Thank you for your trouble." When he hesitated before leaving, I realized he was focused on the widening puddle of seeping snow-melt that I seemed to be neglecting. The story could wait. I called maintenance and started to move books and files to higher ground.

I watched the noon news and the ten o'clock news, but there was no mention of flood victims. "Maybe Larry's safe somewhere," I said to my wife, trusting that outcome not to be considered newsworthy for television.

The flood remained the lead story on Sunday, but the update included the mention of a flood-related death, a body identified as that of an elderly man named Lawrence Abrams being found jammed under a truck in a neighborhood notorious for frequent flooding. "Mr. Abrams, a retired professor, was discovered by a neighbor who had been allowed back onto his property early this morning to retrieve personal items from his evacuated house," the newscaster said. "It appears, authorities have said, as if Mr. Abrams' car stalled in the rushing flood water, and when he stepped out, the current swept him off his feet and under the truck."

My wife and I recognized Larry's house in the short video that followed. There was an interview with a rescue worker, who commented, "I hate to say this, but if Mr. Abrams had not left at all, he could have ridden this out in his home. Plenty of flood damage, sure, but the water, at its worst, would have been only about knee-high inside and he had stairs that led up to an attic."

"The experts told him to leave," I said. Angry, I shut off the television and walked to one of our large, south-facing, living-room windows designed for taking advantage of solar energy. The lights from our house reflected off the pools of water and the leftover snow in the yard in a way that seemed picturesque.

"It's not their fault," my wife said. "He waited a bit too long."

Though she was right, what my wife said made me angrier. "You know what's their fault," I said. "They didn't call him Dr. Abrams. They didn't bother to acknowledge who he was." Though it would make no difference, just then, as I stared out at the remnants of terrible weather, that earned title seemed absolutely important to have been mentioned.

The Nearness of Falling

1

While crossing our town's main street between its two stop lights, a woman is struck by what a witness describes as "a speeding white jeep." Her body is lifted and flung before falling to the pavement near her car. The driver pauses, then flees. Barely, she survives, suffering multiple serious injuries to her legs and internal organs. The newspaper publishes her photograph beside the front-page story. She works at the same university as I do. By the end of the following day, the jeep driver is identified as a man who lives "nearby." There is security camera footage. The police report that they have examined his white jeep. Pending test results that seem to be a formality, he is nearly certain to be arrested.

2

For several years now, each of my doctors' assistants asks, "Have you experienced any recent falls?" A few weeks ago, for the first time, I say "yes," then quickly tense and add, "It's not like you think," hurrying to the anecdote about pulling weeds from the steep bank behind our garage, stepping back, losing my footing, and doing the head-over-heels through specialty grass, a yucca plant, and a patch of iris before rolling across a low stone wall and onto the lawn where I sprawled, taking a minute to evaluate my body from head to toe. I tell her I call myself lucky when the only problem seems to be strained ligaments in my left thumb. When the assistant begins to enter something into her computer, I say, "It's not the kind of fall you're looking for."

3

Overnight, a high school classmate messages our five-year-old fiftieth reunion batch list to observe how the deaths of long-ago friends have become as ordinary as war casualties. She attaches an obituary scanned from a small-town paper, *extended illness* this time, not *suddenly,* not *accident,* further reference to the concealed carry of that classmate's body.

4

When I mention my recent fall to the doctor herself, she says, "It's a slippery slope," not meaning the bank behind my garage. "Mobility limitations often lead to a decline in most things people do. Think of mobility as a barometer for how well you're aging."

After my exam, I follow two patients who seem to have kept appointments together, a husband and wife, most likely, or two friends or neighbors. The man uses a cane, yet struggles along the slight downgrade to the parking lot, holding to the railing with his free hand. The woman relies upon a walker, shuffling beside the opposite railing, not touching it, but appearing to take comfort from having it close by. When I pass, careful to give each one room, they nevertheless stiffen and stop. Later, as I pull away from the clinic, they are still navigating that ramp, and yet there is the sidewalk to cross after the railing ends, and then one of them, because nobody is waiting inside either car parked in the handicapped zone, needs to drive.

5

In the kitchen, sometimes, my wife begins to walk backward, doing short trips between the sink and the table. Mostly, she does those retreats in the living room, happy to have six additional steps of room for the ten minutes of walking backward that a friend has told her helps postpone becoming unsteady. She always musters a smile when she manages back and back again with grace.

6

Nearly seventy-four, an Emeritus Professor, now, for more than two years, I take advantage of the school's fitness room more than I do its library. Even before I retired, I was sure I was the oldest person there every time I went. I go early, the upstairs room full of treadmills, stationary bikes, and elliptical machines, the room below it packed with weighted machinery to exercise every muscle in the body. Mostly, those two rooms are being used by young women. Unless someone remembers me from a years-ago class, no one speaks to me except a few other faculty members. On the level beneath the muscle-toning machines I use, there are thousands of pounds of free weights and music, mostly rap, turned up loud. It's been fifteen years since I hazarded a trip down the stairs to try my hand at the free weights when I knew the room was likely empty at six a.m.

7

A scientist claims that the increased stress of our modern life may be withering the hippocampus. During depression, it seems to shrink, contracting from the drought of optimism. The hippocampus, that scientist says, is so vulnerable to stress that the common names for things it stores might leave their home. Memories become early departures, the ability to make new ones already on red-eyes to where the mind arrives unattended while even the body's fundamentals, tucked deep inside the brain like carefully packaged glassware, show signs of shattering.

8

Thirty-two years ago, when I visited after my mother died, my father wanted to play golf every day the weather permitted. Before we left his house, though he was five years younger than I am now, he wrapped his knees in his unlit bedroom, using fifty years of first aid lessons he'd given to Boy Scout troops he'd led. "Ready?" he would say, a polite request. "I am."

Despite any heat or humidity, he always wore his old work pants. What he complained about was the cart that cost too much, but now was necessary. He never said a word about his knees or his varicose veins or his troubled heart.

9

At my request, my wife agrees to find and walk a long-abandoned section of the Pennsylvania turnpike. Nearly sixty years it's been since several miles of that highway, including two tunnels, were taken out of service. The tunnels, left behind by the railroad, were only two lanes wide, an impossible bottleneck, traffic clogged to a crawl, headlights necessary to fend off fear of oncoming traffic inside them. An alternate section was finally completed. The site, by now, looks like a museum for a post-apocalypse future, the roadway cracked and disintegrating, scrub trees and bushes rearing head high, the two tunnels spawning thousands of graffiti artists and outright vandals. "This is no place to trip and fall," my wife says, the road we begin to walk on vacant for as far as we can see in either direction, our car the only one parked in a small lot a few hundred yards away.

10

For months, the hit-and-run victim is wheelchair bound. Then, for short distances, she is able to use a walker. The newspaper reports there are additional, unspecified complications. Sympathy lingers and sighs before moving on. Soon, she loses the job that made her my colleague for three months. The company that fires her makes the termination call from fifteen hundred miles away.

11

Late last year, my daughter's wedding, her second, was held outdoors in a storied California canyon, the nearest town, a week earlier, evacuated by wildfire, the one access road closed while a community died in flames. A mile north, two days before we arrived, devastation had been declared contained, that metaphorical border unseen by guests. Two days afterward, nearly next for takeoff for our return trip to Pennsylvania, the pilot announced, "Our computer has informed us the plane cannot be flown successfully," and we taxied to the gate, disembarked to wait, then to be rescheduled and vouchered for overnight in a cheap hotel.

12

When I notice my wife walking backward, I agree that the legs are vital, stories of hip-breaking falls already stored on retirement's flash-drive. Friends our age have taken tumbles that force them to begin taking baby steps on level ground, and yet I default to a skepticism that requires me to refuse joining her.

13

A descending ladder of thoughts and prayers follows the post from my high school classmate, the phrase as familiar as the sound of passing traffic. I'm up so early the starlings are just now awakening, every teeming tree chattering what sounds like an invisible babble of surveillance. I add a postscript of my own, all of it referencing events from over fifty-five years ago. Hourly, throughout the late morning and afternoon, I check back. During the evening, as well, but nothing is added, not even more thoughts and prayers.

14

Without exception, the websites I examine say that mobility promotes healthy aging, helping to maintain the ability to live independently and reduce the risk of falling and fracturing bones, helping to maintain healthy muscles, bones and joints, helping to control joint swelling and pain associated with arthritis.

15

In the university fitness room, three gray-haired women appear early each morning to dust and wipe clean the surfaces of machines that measure maintenance. They wear oversized shirts tucked into baggy pants, and when one reaches behind my stationary bike to fine-tune where nobody would notice, I nearly pause to tell her my father, after closing his bakery, became a janitor when he was forty-seven years-old, choosing night shift so he could work alone, his only partner the self-discipline he wore like a uniform to make locker rooms and gymnasiums spotless for coaches and teams he never saw.

16

At another doctor's office three weeks after my fall, the assistant is more specific with her questions after I admit I've fallen: Do you have difficulty climbing up ten steps or walking a quarter of a mile? Because of underlying health or physical reasons, have you modified the way you climb any steps?

It's because of my knees and back, I answer, not because I'm out of breath. She writes my acquiescence into her computer without comment, and I don't mention that my thumb hasn't improved much after weeks have passed.

17

I've learned there is one small solace for those whose brains are failing: the damaged hippocampus might never again make new memories, but older memories are often safe.

18

The hit-and-run victim had once been a dancer. She has children whose accomplishments she mentions to the reporter who writes about her case as the six-month anniversary of her accident arrives. Her friend, the principal witness, says she wants everyone to know they were both sober when the collision occurred. She says there is no question the jeep was traveling way over the speed limit. She says the driver knew what had happened. She says she would know that jeep anywhere. The victim, the article reports, is going to have a series of kidney operations soon.

19

To help study aging, a "handicap suit" has been created at an MIT lab. Nicknamed AGNES, an acronym for "age gain now empathy system," it simulates a variety of issues common to gaining handicaps by including tight bands around the knees to produce stiffness and padded boots to produce loss of tactile feedback. By now, the researchers know that most wearers become angry. The suit infuriates the wearers by slowing and making awkward even the most routine actions.

20

On my father's favorite golf course, the fourteenth hole overlooks an immaculate farm that spreads along the creek that winds through the course. The two of us would sit where I parked the cart in the shade, neither of us mentioning heat or humidity, relying on the view to account for a few minutes of rest. I would wait for him to say, as always, how beautiful it was and then turn away while he pushed himself up and out of the cart with both hands and steadied himself with the five iron he'd pulled from his bag before we parked, then used it as a cane before preparing to carry a hundred and twenty yards over water to the green while I waited, still standing in the shade, with a nine iron.

21

Cautionary Tales:

1. The tomb of Jesus is in danger of collapse. The shrine's foundation is so unstable that an engineering miracle is required for safety.
2. Just off the coast of Australia, four of the stone-tower Apostles have drowned in the sea. Diving is necessary to examine the bodies of the towers that are underwater.
3. From the shore, near San Francisco, a local resident gladly shows me where the famous earthquake's epicenter lies offshore near Mussel Rock.
4. Where I live, thick stone supports are strung across the Susquehanna River, remnants of a bridge collapsed, decades ago, by torrents of ice freed by heavy late-January rain.

22

For more than a decade, my father, his knees ruined to the threat of buckling, crawled backward down the stairs to the damp basement for the years-old jars of my mother's preserves that spoke one version of eternity.

23

Recently, I watched as one fitness room cleaning woman began to vacuum the carpet and another squatted to clean an exercise mat She settled, at last, for sitting within a fog of sighs. Two minutes after she finished and struggled to her feet, a student in matching shorts and tank-top wiped that mat with a white, antiseptic cloth before lowering herself to stretch her toned body while what sounded like static reached me from pale, blue buds pressed into the student's ears. The student's rapt listening was as visible as the vacuum cleaner tracks I followed moments later, staying inside one narrow swatch as if it overlooked a brief, but fatal fall.

24

Five weeks after my daughter's wedding, for our long-planned retreat from winter in Pennsylvania, my wife and I return to Los Angeles. Our January rental is on the twelfth floor of a building a mile from our daughter's residence, only the penthouse above us. "Like we're near the stars," our young granddaughters say when both of them follow my wife, later that evening, onto the balcony to watch her lean over the railing to photograph the rare, red moon while I stay behind, dizzy with imagined falling, yet three full steps from any chance of tumbling over the railing.

The elevator, each day, always rises to meet us. If there are passengers, they always disembark on our floor. For all we know, the penthouse lies empty. Four weeks, it takes, for the elevator to descend when we press the down call-button. The passengers are an elderly couple, the woman white-haired, illness-thin, and immaculately dressed. When we greet them, the woman speaks over our heads as if fixed upon the descending numbers. After we settle at the lobby floor, her right hand flutters toward the man in a way that confirms she is blind or very nearly so. One hand on her back and one gripping her arm, he talks her slowly across the lobby toward a luxury car, shuffling in sync with her tiny, cautious steps.

25

When, after months, the hit-and-run victim is released from the hospital, a donor volunteers a motorized scooter that, he says, had been a life-saver for him. The gift-giver, in the newspaper's large photo, looks bent and fragile. In a jaunty font, Pride Go-Go is splashed across the scooter's side. The donor's hand rests on a handlebar as if he relies upon it for balance.

26

For a week, I check the class reunion site, but the thread still ends with my comment. However, a new one begins—an old classmate has posted to explain how mindfulness was such a godsend during her career as a professor. She says she used to practice "feeling" to prepare for the end-of-semester trauma of failing students. She says she the technique became even more important when she rehearsed for her mother's passing, that now she calculates the responses to her own death by remembering herself in the third person. Upstairs, two doors slam. A few hours later, my old classmate returns to post she has listened, minutes before, to a recording of giraffes in a Viennese zoo. Though everyone believes they are mute, she writes, they hum to each other at night, the frequency so low nobody noticed. For comfort, she guesses, for reassurance, though she acknowledges that scientists are, for now, uncertain.

27

Twenty-two years ago, after knee surgery, I submitted to the cajoling of a therapist who set the treadmill, initially, at one mph. My hands gripped the railings while I relearned the alphabet of walking. Across the room was a patient who seemed unable to stand. From a nearby apparatus, another patient whispered my way, "It's hell, ain't it?"

28

For his eighty-fifth birthday, I drove my father to the property he'd bought while believing he could make a life there with my mother after he closed his small bakery. I was thirteen, so I know he was forty that year. He thought ten years would free him to part-time work, the self-sufficiency of livestock and well-tended fields. My sister and I would be gone by then, whatever money he had enough for two people happy with little.

The dirt lane, unchanged, took us past the house he'd rented out but never lived in, winding to a field he asked me to drive into, following some farmer's matted meadow tracks to the edge of the wooded acres he'd loved. I shortened my steps as he limped slowly among the trees to where we could see, still standing, a shelter he'd built by hand the year

I was twenty, preparing for picnics, the families my sister and I would bring each summer. I held my father's hand against the threat of roots and rocks until he stuttered the last small steps to the shelter. Beyond a patch of pines, a man smoked on the porch beside the rented house, and I worried he'd seen us until he bent to busy himself with a shovel. My father ran his hands over the logs he'd raised to form a room no one, apparently, had used in years. When he asked me to try the door, I pressed until it buckled inward on the covered space, where, he said, he wanted to stand, knowing it had lasted.

29

After a year, the newspaper revisits the hit-and-run story. The test results on the jeep, according to the police spokesperson, are still incomplete. He asks for patience. Near the accident site, a few flowers are strewn. The following morning, they are gone, either gathered and saved or simply picked up and discarded.

30

My wife knows that I pedal in the fitness room not only as a way to stay fit and maintain mobility, but also to relieve depression. She doesn't know that I spin my digital pulse into the age-calibrated red zone, a range that was marked "conditioning" ten years ago. That before backing off, I am both terrified and thrilled.

31

Cautionary Tales:

1. To pilgrims, the temple constructed at the site of Christ's tomb must have made heaven seem near, yet it's been destroyed and restored three times.
2. Mussel Rock, the writer John McPhee writes, is like a three-story building standing in the Pacific, with brown pelicans on the roof where the San Andreas Fault intersects the sea.
3. The remaining Apostles, because they are made of limestone, will be extinguished by the sea. In time, the sea will create more by carving them from the current cliffs.

4. The damaged bridge, unrepaired, stands like a monument to instability.

32

In a study conducted by the makers of a personal emergency response system, the alarm button that hung around my father's neck for nearly five years, 83% of subscribers who fell and couldn't get up for more than five minutes didn't use the alarm, most likely because they didn't want anyone to know about their helplessness. During all those years my father wore that alarm, despite his history of falls, the only time his alarm button was pushed was by his curious great-grandson.

33

In the newspaper, a physical therapist is interviewed about the mobility issues of the elderly. "If you are unable to get out and around," she says, "you can't go shopping or out with friends to eat dinner or go to the movies, and you become dependent on other people to get you places. You are likely to become a recluse. You stay home and get depressed. With immobilization comes incontinence, because you can't get to the bathroom. Then you can develop urinary infections and skin infections. It's like a row of falling dominoes."

34

After two years, the hit-and-run victim completes extensive kidney surgery, one of them removed. The test results on the white jeep are still in limbo, even as the statute of limitations is about to expire. Along our main street, a church has filled a vacant storefront. On folding chairs, a small congregation, each Sunday, sits as quietly as the truth. The hit-and-run victim is reported to be moving to Turkey.

35

Before boarding for our most recent flight to California, I am pulled aside for a stand-and-frisk. The guard pats me down, carefully tracing the corrugated surface of my leg as other travelers, curious, retrieve the items they carry close. He pauses by my knee to ask what it is he feels. "Varicose veins," I say. He offers me his screen, my image bright yellow from below the knee to mid-thigh, a sign, he says, that suggests knee replacement, smuggling, or even a suicide bomb. We shake hands. He even smiles, "They must hurt," he says, and I walk away assessing imperfection's power, just one of the terrorists we might travel with, those raised and bubbled veins so much like multiple fuses that flight must be preceded by the self-incrimination of the body.

36

For the hour my wife and I hike along the near rubble of the stretch of abandoned turnpike, the sound of traffic along the nearby open stretch of road is constant. For a brief time, the cars and trucks can even be seen through a section of sparse foliage. We are frightened by the approach of the only two people we see. Both men prove to be friendly, stopping to chat, asking what they might expect to discover next. However, when they vanish, we worry again about their possible intentions. As if even among so much disuse and decay, we can still doubt that anyone but us could be interested simply in finding synonyms for collapse.

37

My dermatologist examines me literally from the top of my head to between my toes. Yesterday, as she looked closely at my legs, she paused at my varicose veins. "Does it hurt?" she said.

38

As we retrace our steps along the abandoned stretch of highway, my wife and I pass the place where we can see the turnpike traffic through the trees. "Do you think any of them are aware?" she says, and though I have no way of knowing for certain, I answer "No."

39

After three years, word arrives that the hit and run victim has died. The cause is reported as cancer; a rumor has it by an opioid overdose. For certain is the news that she had won a settlement in civil court for $50,000, what seems a tiny, unacceptable sum. The parents of the suspected driver had paid in exchange for no admission of guilt on their son's part. The suspect who will never be tried is twenty-three now, his residence less than a mile from the accident site. The victim's children flew to Turkey to oversee her burial. The store-front congregation has grown in size. From the street, when they are repeating their litanies, they seem to be stage-whispering reassurances: "And still." "And yet." "Despite that," the code cadenced into the weakening heartbeat of epitaph.

40

My father, at ninety, was interested only in the sound of my voice, caulking each pause with "good," his legs restless in a wheelchair.

41

Now I am afraid, some days, that I, too, am growing indifferent to things. There are mornings when loss of interest extends an overnight visit, as if I should check the bedroom closet for a rack of foreign clothes, the hamper for strange underwear, the bathroom where I believe I might find an extra toothbrush, a display of prescription medicines, a towel damp at six a.m., the shower stall traced with fog.

42

Last evening, when my wife walked backward, I joined her, both of us counting our steps together without feeling behind ourselves for the bookcase or the wall devoted to art, doing a simple line dance to the rhythm of apprehension's melody, hearing time's chorus hummed into our ears, the one so familiar we automatically mouth the lyrics, walking backward to its music, following the lead that waltzes us in a tempo so comfortable we barely sense the tiny increments of change, and balance seems enough for joy.

Isolation

A day without news. Left behind, last night's lead story—a friend's untimely death, his son surviving the head-on two miles from home. This evening, my near-misses an embarrassment of luck inherited like wealth. Three times, after our father died, my sister sent half of his years-hidden stash of bonds, CDs, or even cash that was never enough for news.

My friend believed the news was a woman so beautiful he would never tire of her body. It was like his love of drinking, returning daily to that desire, sometimes seeking my company for an evening that extended toward the blackout of any sort of news.

Maybe that need is a form of loneliness that catches in the throat like a concealed confession for the disquiet of restraint, a moment when we are, at least, in understanding's vicinity. Outside, three steep miles of trail descend through forest. Apprehensive, who wouldn't reminisce for comfort?

At 20:45, April 18, 1930, the Wagner on the BBC, as scheduled, was interrupted for fifteen minutes of news. Those listening to the radio were worried, most likely, about financial affairs, the way the world was teetering toward another war, but they heard "There is no news," and a piano began to play as if nothing outside of their lives had happened, and they could speak to each other softly as the piano continued, their living rooms the extent of what mattered enough to record and repeat, something like the somber music after Kennedy's assassination, each station suddenly gone to cathedral organs, bagpipes, and military bands, all the instrumental ways to indicate the news of loss in the interlude between death and its details through the static of a distant station or the hum that lives between frequencies.

In 1930, within radio's community, every listener was intent upon the first sign of interruption, importance loitering outside, even as the Wagner returned, an aria at 21:00 without the solace of excuses. One by one, those listeners shifted in their chairs and began to whisper as a woman cried beautifully in song about unrequited desire.

Consolations

From day to day, second to second, the self preserves itself, clinging to that instrument: time, the instrument that it was supposed to play.

—Walter Benjamin

1

At two, my son loved his car seat. Like a dog, he scrambled up to watch anything fly past. Each time I shifted lanes, reeling in a truck, he repeated, "go" and "fast," chanting a chorus of his love for speed. I laughed sometimes, but I knew that, like a dog, he would, if he weren't harnessed in that seat, thrust his head out that window. Maybe, I sometimes thought, he'd be so excited he'd push himself so far outside that he'd tumble, one unspoken reason I double-checked the clips that kept him sitting. The alternative I imagined was something for which there would be no consolation.

2

A woman I once met said she could never imagine being consoled after losing a swimmer while lifeguarding. Hand-over-hand, a boy had edged to deep water along the dock that claimed part of a lake for summer camp. No matter the reason, he'd lost his grip and gone under while she'd scolded another boy for running, adding a minute between her whistles for buddy checks. "Last warning," she'd said to the running boy. "Don't let me see that again."

For seventeen years now, she said, her dreams were often whistles and screams. Always, there was water-with-shadow, a still life framed by memory's limits. She woke with what felt like heavy weight yoked by her arms. Twice each night, she rose to check the breathing of her children who slept paired in two rooms. A trilling in her ears insisted that she evaluate the pillows, examine the chests for the relief of rise and fall.

What I didn't tell her was that I'd practiced CPR, once, on a dummy called Mike Muscles, bringing him back from the dead with my hands and breath. Imagine yourself watching a boy dragged from a swimming pool, the instructor had said. Imagine your well-trained hands on his chest was the only way to resurrect him.

After that woman had walked away, I evaluated how hungry I was, sometimes, for a story to spew at acquaintances, believing that sort of appetite was widely shared. For once I said nothing. Safety is impossible. There is never shame in the inability to comfort.

3

For a second time, I am returning in writing to the afternoon, on a stretch of freeway so familiar that safety seemed routine, I began to pass a tractor trailer. During a moment within the trucker's blind spot or his carelessness, the semi pulled left, and I punched the brakes, locking my small car into a four-wheel drift up and over the shallow median into the two oncoming lanes of that highway, still braking until I stuck to the opposite wide shoulder, facing traffic like the highway patrol.

Three cars slowed, a small truck dawdled, drivers and passengers gawking. I didn't thank God for perfectly spacing the high-speed traffic. I waited for a clear stretch across all four lanes and humped over the median to finish my trip, accepting my exit where that truck still idled at a stoplight. I watched as the driver opened his door and walked past five cars to signal me to open my window. When I did, he said, "I'll bet you're sitting in it" and reached in to offer his hand.

I said "No" so calmly and so softly, it must have sounded something like gratitude for his appreciation of my peril. The light turned green while that trucker held his handshake, both of us ignoring the horns of that lengthening line of cars.

When I told my wife what had happened on that routine drive to the college campus where I was an entry-level English instructor, she stayed silent until I mentioned the driver's handshake. "That was some consolation," I said, "having him admit he felt so guilty."

"I'm glad you're safe," she said, "but the real consolation is your son wasn't in the car with you," she said.

4

Facebook posts routinely plead, "Send thoughts and prayers," and because so many readers are alone or anxious or accept the power of such comfort, dozens of comments begin "dear God" and "prayers sent," phrases as familiar as passing traffic, the highway just far enough from my house they are erased by a gibberish of wind and starlings awakening. Upstairs, when even the predawn hours are hot, the skylights are open to crosswind, ceiling fans spinning sluggishly, nearly as helpless as the cardboard ones provided by the church my father once required, no excuses. They opened and shut like accordions, pictures of Jesus delivering the Sermon on the Mount, blessing the loaves and fishes, healing the sick, or kneeling in prayer in the Garden of Gethsemane. All summer, they were scattered along each pew where new hymnals, one Sunday the year I turned fifteen, were distributed, all of them purchased, I learned through opening and shutting as many as I could during the following months, to honor the memory of somebody's loved one. Those hymnals also contained a table that listed the dates when Easter would occur for each of the next sixty-five years. The last of those dates, impossibly far away, was 2025, embedded in an April for which science has prophesied worldwide coastal flooding, the city in which I was reading those forecasts abandoned like a shopping mall where, after dark, a dread of cars idles without headlights.

5

Because my mother died on New Year's Day, because I visited to comfort my father, who refused to move any of her things, I saw how Christmas had stalled at gifts unwrapped but not unpacked, how her medicine had been arranged by frequency: Crystodigin, Aldomet (once daily), Cytomel (three times per day). They supported her weak heart, and I lifted the vial of Percocet (as needed, for severe pain, no refills) and wondered at the gaps between the demands that had been screamed by my mother's heart. Beside it was Nitrostat (as needed, for chest pain), those pills that the foolish in movies always grope toward as they collapse while still one room from relief, the urgency of those labels convinced me that my mother would surely have understood they represented a hierarchy of help from which she would not emerge.

During my visit, I learned that my father had been taking blood pressure medicine for years, keeping that need closeted as if it were shameful. By then, I had issues of my own that required tablets I took, twice daily; capsules I swallowed, as needed; and vapor I breathed in the lapsed-lung darkness, lying back like Proust, whose life I'd learned for my job. His asthma, however, bedded him for years. He insisted, finally, a huge black woman was chasing him. For sure, she caught him.

Each morning, my father strained to speak, beginning, "Well, did you sleep good?" and I answered him, "Good enough" as if the truth might trigger prescriptions, as if accidentally we might talk, as needed, to console our faulty selves.

After dinner that night, my father led me outside. The falling snow was nothing but an hour's cover. When we walked across my father's yard, the grass returned where our shoes pressed. "There's my sky," he said," and not knowing what he expected, I answered, standing in his driveway, "It's clear all right." I stared upward, thinking my father was planning to tell me about the ancient names for the stars or the tales they inspired about people who suffered and changed and ascended while somebody left behind handed his story down to another generation. The two dippers and Orion were all I could remember and locate, and I waited for him to show me where he believed my mother was, how one cluster of stars had reformed, at least for him, to suggest a melodrama of hope. The two of us stood with the night in our lungs. We breathed a sentence of silence until he said, "Venus and Jupiter," directed me low in the sky where there were so many lights I could nod, certain they were among them.

6

After that near-miss on the highway, the present open-carried a blind spot. When my son sat behind me, clouds seemed to be crossing the lifeline of the sky's palm. *Lost control* sprouted on billboards along every four-lane highway like PAC-bought posters for candidates I despised.

When to pass a truck became a formal question. Likewise, how. I loved their uphill crawls that made passing easy, but for miles, sometimes, there were curves and downhill slopes that postponed the extended seconds of side-by-side.

For a while, my wife admired my caution. She nodded at where our young son was sitting and said that it was good to see me being a father when I drove. He grew into his new outfit of sentences while I kept my brush with impermanence secret.

7

Her cries enhanced by the dorm wall echo, the student sitting in the stairwell weeps. A step above stands the boy who must have shown her that love is as perishable as groceries stamped with shelf-life warnings. She raises her hand to her face. Without skipping a sob, she lets me climb. Wary at public sorrow, the boy holds his stance.

Even when I paused like an eavesdropper, I tell a colleague later, she didn't lift her head. My colleague says "aboulia" as if I should recognize a strange, ancient word for that tableau. He's spent much of his lifetime studying the obsolete and archaic, certain there are words that fit so exactly to feeling they transcend the narratives for ambivalence, anxiety and angst. When he's satisfied he has me puzzled, he says, "Think of how she's sitting there like you say. It shows loss of volition." He waits a beat and adds, "Loss of will," grinning as if he owns an antonym to extract from obscurity, the word that would define my bald neighbor coughing up mucus beside the hybrid sapling he carried to the hole I'd dug for what he insisted would flourish faster than sumac, swelling to shade my new house, what, statistically, he is unlikely to witness despite his latest experimental cancer therapy. Or my father, his knees ruined to the threat of buckling, crawling backward down the stairs to the flood-prone basement for the years-old jars of my mother's preserves that speak one version of eternity.

8

Once, in May, a tractor near where I lived in western New York vanished beneath the earth, a farmer too early into the onion fields.

I stared at the John Deere, large and green, as it rose from the mud, heaved up by pulleys. Those of us watching were told that the farmer, as his tractor sank, had stood, riding until his shoes had touched the soil, becoming, he'd said, a temporary Jesus, walking away from the disbelief of drowning.

One of my students, fifteen that spring, had lost an eye in a farm accident several years earlier. The empty socket had been stitched closed; her hair always hung across nearby scars like cloth. Nobody knew whether or not she would receive an artificial eye or plastic surgery. I was told that she'd been piggyback riding her father, her thin legs still pale in early May, hugging his neck in shorts and t-shirt, a model for the joy of family farming. The story another teacher told me included these details: Her father's black Harvester had flushed birds and turned over two nests of mice before it bucked and tossed her. I didn't ask him how he knew that.

That summer, a boy my older son's age tumbled under the harrow that trailed his father's red New Holland. A minister said, "Remember the eight years of joy that child has brought," as if the dead boy were that farmer's pet. After the service, the one-eyed girl followed her father, whose shoulders were so hunched he appeared to be dragging her.

In September, the girl with one eye said she loved unhappy endings because everyone deserved misery. By then, my last year as a high school teacher, I was a ghost who often left the school before I re-entered my body and walked home to my wife and three children who had not been injured, their tragedies postponed. To walk off dissatisfaction, some afternoons I chose a longer, indirect route home. A few times, I passed tractors idling near fields to be harvested. Twice, farmers crouched beside them as if in thought.

9

I have been reading about scientific fraud, cases of men and women altering their data to make it fit their hopes for success. The well-known obstetrician, for example, who published a research paper in the *British Journal of Obstetrics and Gynecology*, claiming that a 29-year-old woman had given birth to a healthy baby after he had successfully relocated a five-week-old ectopic fetus into her womb, a report that raised the hopes of women prone to pregnancies that start outside the uterus and end in miscarriage. Patient records, however, had been tampered with, suspicion resting upon the obstetrician. Moreover, colleagues knew nothing about the case he was referencing, and the mother could not be found. The doctor had falsified everything. One other patient, in fact, was already dead when he claimed to have operated on her.

Years ago, six miles from where I live, a skeleton was unearthed from the bank of the Susquehanna River, each day regaining more of itself from dental work and the evidence of wounds. The newspaper published photographs of the long-missing woman, interviews with her mother. It's the end of uncertainty, she said. The end of miracles, she added, when the story continued on an inside page. Beside that report, the newspaper ran a photograph of a woman displaying one thousand origami cranes she owned in order to bring fulfillment of wishes. Which made me think, for a moment, that there is some reason to forgive the scientists who have altered data, the researchers with their "golden hands." Absolve the man who marked mice with the ink of false verification. Pardon the doctor who beat probability with a simple shift of answers. For they do the work of our wishes. For they bring miracles and divine intervention. There are so many God signs in science we need a library for likely fraud, space enough for enormous paper flocks to dream among, those frail, paper birds so securely settled, they will not startle.

10

One evening, when I was in the car alone, no headlights behind me, two deer dashed across that near-accident highway. I braked hard and veered, this time maintaining control. In the rearview mirror, I watched them reach the opposite shoulder as if, in some invisible spectrum, I had been the only driver to run the traffic light that signaled them to cross.

The following day, marking the months-old moment of my miracle, I parked where and when I skidded. I stood beside my car and prepared to non-stop cross. Three minutes, it took, for me to believe even a sprinter's space had opened. I waited another minute, then nearly turned an ankle as I ran across the median. Gravel coughed under my shoes when I braked on the far shoulder, blinking, a few seconds later, against the grit blown up by the first oncoming truck.

11

The pet cemetery near Stroudsburg was the kind of place I walked with a notebook, a grant supporting me across Pennsylvania. I copied down inscriptions that read like parodies and wondered what anyone driving Route 80 would think of Edgar Friedell paying somebody to inscribe *Bambi Was My Baby* on a headstone. I thought of how I was spending Pennsylvania's money, believing I could find poems or stories daily by starting my car. I remembered the fat anthologies I carried, the number of fellowship winners like myself who filled up American highways until they found one place that convinced them they were alone in a particular inspiration. I walked down past *Our Lost Little Girlie* and *My Sweetie* and stood on the shoulder of the highway the way, as a boy, I had often done to hitchhike before I thought about poems and stories or even how much one of those drivers could have made me pay for accepting a ride, and I kept guessing how I looked to every man or woman who might be watching for hitchhikers, wanting to heave that notebook across all four lanes of Route 80, one more tax dollar symbol, wishing for Edgar Friedell to show up with flowers so I could ask him how he'd done it, loved something enough to sign his name.

12

Thirty years ago, shortly after I began teaching creative writing at another university, one of my students died in a campus accident. Afterward, I rewrote, in cursive, a few lines from her workshop poem about the possibilities of love, listening to the imagery for desire with intricate loops and decisive slants. Her setting is a garden dedicated to St. Paul tended by two ancient nuns who, each day, inspect the light altered by arrangements of decorative trees; who prune, monthly, the rose bushes to allow kneeling before the raised right hand of a smiling Mary. Pausing, I remembered it had been years since I had noticed a nun. Because they have abandoned their habits, I decided, and remembered how they rode the streetcar in pairs when I was a boy; how they gathered at the museum where I was transfixed by dinosaur bones, mummies, and animals stuffed and mounted.

My student's sixteen lines detailed blossoms that flourished like sacrifice; they added topiary that shadowed erosions from frequent storms, the nuns often singing. I recalled Soeur Sourire, the Singing Nun, her song about Dominique relentless on the radio, her Ed Sullivan minutes, how I followed her brief career, discovering she had left the order for a woman, nothing certain by then but the pull of desire.

The priest who blessed my wedding fled the church for a woman who had spent seven years as a nun. Soon Sister Smile killed herself, nuns becoming improbable as faith. My student, at last, shifted to the white statue of the garden saint, her blessed hand smooth from centuries of kisses, her poem ending in an astonishment of prayer.

13

What I had no heart for, the day I ran across the freeway, was the return dash. I looked both ways and calculated. I hesitated. I stuttered and stopped and decided to wait until the traffic was so clear I could cover four lanes by walking. Four lanes distant, my car appeared to be abandoned, as if it would soon be stripped by opportunistic thieves.

14

My father, his collection of canes arranged against a wall, accepted, at last, the walker and the nursing home. Ninety, he shuffled and imagined intruders and thieves who believed stealth obsolete in the room of the deaf. Hourly each night, he struggled to the bathroom in darkness, sure he would welcome them, wolves come to rescue him from the wheelchair, from the hospital bed, the catheter's humiliation of extended care.

One Saturday afternoon, we rode the nursing home's elevator down to the chapel where I guided him to the stained-glass window he'd donated, twenty years before, in memory of my mother. After the window had been installed, he'd driven me thirty miles to see it, asking, when we'd entered, "Which one? Guess." When I chose flowers and doves, a setting suggesting what he expected of paradise, he was pleased enough to say, "Good" and wave me close to read the inscription.

When those birds and lilies caught the low sun, they seemed transfigured by eternity. "Look," I said, hearing the light of expectation in my voice. My father stared and waited as if he were listening for me to go on, but I kept my sense of accidental symbolism to myself. He leaned on his walker so close to the identification plaque that he laid his hand upon it as he needed to map my way to understanding. "See?" he said, "to Ruthy," as if that inscription were a miracle.

15

A lifelong friend has retired to South Carolina. Last spring, while we crossed the bridge to return from a resort island restaurant, my friend's wife, driving slowly, said, "Here is where the accident occurred," describing carelessness, inattention, and a driver texting while veering over the median and so much as murdering a woman she knew well, the husband injured but recovering, by now, for several months. "Because she was driving," my friend said. "Because, like me, he sees poorly at night."

The following morning, that crash survivor, unannounced, joined my friend and me for golf. I shook his hand when we met, and though I carried my knowledge of his secret misery like an extra club, the truth is I prepared, if needed, a sentence of consolation, that for three and a half hours I thought I was being asked to prove who I was and became, at best, another retiree come south in winter and easily forgotten. Afterward, over beer, I told my friend I felt like I was spying in a changing room.

This year, visiting again, I learned that widower never played another round with anyone my friend knew, that he'd moved to another state to be close to his children or to be far from the source of suffering, as if distance were a way to peace, a door to bolt against the visitor who never leaves, who does its laundry late at night and leaves crumbs for which no one confesses.

16

One morning, six months after the catastrophe that missed me, as my wife and I were dressing for the day, our young son, as he often did, used our bed for a trampoline. He loved bouncing and flopping, his arms and legs extended into a stick-man pose. We smiled and occasionally clapped until he flopped just far enough forward to slam his face into the headboard. Blood spurted from his forehead. He wailed. My wife pressed a clean towel against the wound and carried him to the car. Within minutes we were in the emergency room.

A young nurse encased him in something that was a hybrid of mummy wrappings and straight-jacket, but our son was already so quiet he seemed to sense that being still was important. When the doctor was finished with the stitches, the nurse, meaning to console us, said the scar would be smaller than we might think, that the damage was so near his hairline that it was unlikely to be noticed. "Unless you give him a crew cut," she said, smiling. The doctor, more serious, said, "Of all the places on his face to damage, this was the best." He paused before he added, "By far" as if he was emphasizing a definition.

On the drive home, my wife and I talked about how grateful we both were, though it came to me that the feeling was temporary because this was not the last time for accident or age or malice to demand some degree of consolation that would never be enough.

On Location: A Valentine

At Griffith Park a few weeks ago, while I tried to convince my granddaughter that hitting a backhand wasn't difficult, she told me that Emma Stone played tennis for a *Battle of the Sexes* scene on a nearby Los Angeles court where her friend takes lessons. "Down by the fountain," she said, meaning the Riverside courts a half mile from where she lives. "The director," she explained, "needed an old-fashioned surface, something that looks like it's in the '70s."

She'd played four times by then, three of them with me, beginning with balls so pressureless they seemed to hover in the air. I told her I was seventeen years older than Bobby Riggs was when he lost to Billie Jean King in the Astrodome, a year younger than Billie Jean was in the present where I was teaching her despite my ruined knees and spinal stenosis and a one-handed backhand that puzzled her.

She wanted to know how hard it was for me to play with a wooden racket, a thing so strange and heavy, its small sweet spot that must have made tennis more difficult. When I said I'd once used a Jack Kramer model, she told me he was the movie's sexist bad guy.

She loved tennis now, planned to use her own money to buy a vintage outfit like the one Emma Stone wears to play Steve Carrell's version of Bobby Riggs. Better yet, she was ready to turn her shoulders early and prepare to swing like Emma Stone, who, like her, had never played until starring in that movie made her learn how Billie Jean King had bounced a ball before serving and how she had held her wooden racket, switching from a forehand to backhand grip.

We were practicing because my daughter had told her I'd coached a college team and spent a few summers as a teaching pro at a country club where successful men, during those 70s, had hired me to teach their wives not to be liabilities in the business of mixed doubles, berating them, sometimes, like minor-league versions of the Jack Kramer she had so much disliked when she'd watched the film.

The court we were using is built into a landscape of rugged, low mountains, a twenty-minute uphill walk from where my wife and I stayed for the month of January. Six times we made that trek, and every time we talked the whole way up and down, most of the time about her current life as a fourteen-year-old.

Two miles above those courts is the observatory where James Dean faced off with the "hoods" in *Rebel Without a Cause*. Two miles below them is the high school James Dean and Natalie Wood, as alienated teenagers, attended in that movie. She is a freshman there, and doesn't imagine herself in the '50s.

My daughter drove me to the Riverside courts a few days later. We stood on the court where Emma Stone pretended to be Billie Jean King winning a tournament held in San Diego. Less than 100 yards away a row of power lines towered up from where they follow US 5 and the roar of heavy Los Angeles traffic.

My granddaughter could walk to that court in ten minutes and play in the footsteps of Emma Stone. She has a forehand now, sometimes a backhand, and less often an accurate serve.

What I kept to myself were the secrets of the once deadly slice of Bobby Riggs, who was born the same year as my father, who, on courts far from Hollywood, taught me what he could from his repertoire of homemade strokes until he handed me to a stranger who changed everything but my backhand, the stroke he said was "a natural."

On the last night of our stay, my granddaughter and I watched *Battle of the Sexes* together, sitting side by side on the couch. She concentrated as if she hadn't already seen it. At last, she said, "Look, there it is, the court," and we watched Emma Stone run across the '70s court, swing her wooden racket, and deliver the illusion of a winning forehand before we said a half hour of goodbyes, we hugged three times, she cried, and I almost did myself.

New Year's Eve, Los Angeles

Because my granddaughter is fifteen, my company is necessary for each mile-long walk to care for two dogs and a cat. Because her street, the last hundred yards of our walk, feels dangerous for anyone. Because the street is really an alley and badly lit. Because there are budget apartments that sit below the narrow street on one side rather than more single-dwelling houses and duplexes like the ones set into the hillside on the right.

The new year is four hours away when we leave the apartment my wife and I have rented for six weeks to avoid winter and visit with our recently remarried daughter. She has saved her honeymoon week until we were available to watch over her daughters. The only complication has been those animals need attention three times a day.

Half way through those last hundred yards, an empty car is double parked in the alley, the driver's side door open. Lights extinguished, a curiosity so close to her house. My granddaughter veers right, and I drift her way as subtly as I can muster. The next bend takes us into the street's deepest shadows just before the flight of stairs to the door.

"Those apartments are sketchy," she says, when we are inside. The dogs welcome us. They go out the back door and soon return, expecting food. The cat, as always, refuses to be seen.

In the bedroom my granddaughter shares with her twelve-year-old sister, we play records I've sent her for Christmas, used albums of mine from the '70s I've guessed she'd love—Queen, Judy Collins, Linda Ronstadt, Harry Neilson—thinning my collection and building hers. We spend an hour with the music, including an entire side of *Nilsson Schmilsson* that my granddaughter sings softly along to. The dogs, instead of settling, are restless, pacing to windows and back to us. Neither of them barks.

As soon as we walk around the bend, beginning the return trip, we see two police cars by the double-parked car, its door still open, but now a young woman is inside. Except for the policeman who waves to invite us past, whoever arrived in those two marked cars must be inside.

"What you looking at, bitch?" the woman says. The policeman's wave shifts into demand. "That's it, keep walking, bitch," the woman calls as we pass him. "Fuck you, bitch," she yells as we clear the scene.

"I wish I hadn't looked," my granddaughter says when we reach the busy highway at the end of her street. "Did you look?"

"Yes."

"But she only talked to me."

I think of comforting or explaining, but settle for, "You'll never see her again." We have nearly a mile for the return walk, but all the rest is where traffic, even on the holiday, is constant. Because we both know there are fewer shadows on the other side, we wait at the first intersection, an awkward one, three streets intersecting the main highway, a series of left turn lights extending the wait. Down the sidewalk on our side, we can see a small crowd has gathered where the apartments have a lower entrance.

"The dogs knew, didn't they?" my granddaughter says, after we have crossed.

"Yes, they must have sensed when the police arrived."

Back in the apartment, we stay up for the bells and sirens and fireworks from a thousand yards spreading toward the city. My granddaughter and I, both terrified of heights, choose to stay inside when my wife and her sister step out on the twelfth-floor balcony. They look like they are in terrible danger, like they could vanish when the railing they lean on collapses. "What do you think she could have done?" my granddaughter says. Before I can answer, she adds, "She didn't look much older than I am," whispering as if it were a secret.

Butterflies, Biopsies, the Lockdown Hosts

If a butterfly flaps its wings in Brazil, it might produce a tornado in Texas.
—The Laws of Chaos

The Butterfly Effect

Once, early in your weekly newsmagazine, a photograph of Haitian women wailing. On the next page, more women who looked to be holding their breath and the hands of men tense with what was identified as "bullet expectations." This was decades ago, the same week you discovered that the wind swirling winter rain along your street might have originated from their mourning, the beating, weeks before, of their arms in the air sending a record warm front north.

You absorbed the Butterfly Effect, how chaos is not chaos, how slaughter in Haiti could flap its wings and churn into your grip on the arm of your son and your hiss through clenched teeth as he fluttered his free arm and wailed and altered, in turn, the future of weather in a country farther east where another father would choose to stun his young son to obedience. That night, after you allowed the dog to walk you into sense, the wind chattered branches that skittered her to a barking panic on your street of sculpted shrubbery where a web of Christmas bulbs, in one nearby yard, might have arranged itself into words if you were properly angled, upstairs, across the street and positioned like an antenna straining for a distant station, like your son behind his bedroom window watching you soft-handle the dog, your breath without its winter clouds, nothing he would believe could join the southern grief of a warm front.

1

Your newest neighbor is a prison guard. His daughter, last summer, came to your door in tears. She sat in your living room and said only that she needed a place to wait, forgetting her key and her curfew time, well past late at twilight. Ten years old, she sipped water your wife offered, her pink shirt covered with butterflies. While waiting for her mother to return her call, she confessed that her father was inside the house, that locked out in the dark was a lesson she was expected to learn, crying on her porch a sentence meant to deter, but this time, a recidivist, she had decided to escape to the closest door that stood open.

2

Your granddaughter's letters from Los Angeles always end with butterflies. One of her drawings, this time, is half a page large, and you are sketched inside both of its wings. Like a species pattern, you think, blue-masked, with red and white dots along your arms and legs, the butterfly a blaze of orange and yellow, the antennae green.

3

Last December, just before the first report from Wuhan slipped into the newspaper, you postponed an ultrasound appointment because it fell on the same day as the one that completed your follow-ups to back surgery. It had been seven years since your first and second thyroid "growths" had been biopsied, ten months apart, both coming up benign. After five years of annual ultrasounds, all of them declaring "stable," you had been put on a two-year cycle, so long between appointments, you had forgotten the latest one and double-scheduled. The decision was easy. The back surgery was recent, the ultrasound a routine precaution.

Because you have spent most of the winter in California, you have an imaging-center appointment for early March. The ultrasound is quick, almost pleasurable. A few days later, a call left on your phone says that one of the two "nodules" has shown significant growth. For years, they have kept their uneasy truce, but now one has swollen like a militia covertly arming. The message ends by announcing that an appointment for the following week has been made for another biopsy.

4

After your parents moved your family into a new house when you were seven, leaving the three-room rental behind, your father hung two framed butterfly collections on the basement wall. He had received a merit badge for that project when he was thirteen, and now he had room for those butterflies to be displayed. He would live in that house for fifty-six years, the last twenty-one years alone, and those butterflies remained exactly where they began. By the time he moved to a nursing home, those butterflies, all of them monarchs, were seventy-seven years old.

5

Due to the Covid-19 pandemic, the hospital postpones your biopsy. When you call your doctor, an automated message says the office is now closed. Your wife tells you that the postponement is good news, that if the doctor thought your tumor was malignant, he would declare the biopsy an emergency and keep it scheduled. "It's just a precaution," she says, but all you hear are the words tumor and malignant. All you see is your mother wearing a wig when you came home from college for Thanksgiving. The site of her "troubles" was her thyroid.

6

"We barely know anything about the new neighbors," your wife said after you both watched the girl in the butterfly shirt walk to where her mother parked in her driveway and waited beside her car. "All those years in classrooms taught me that you can't always trust a child's story when they find themselves into trouble."

7

After your granddaughter sends another butterfly drawing, your wife tells you that Denise, a book club friend, loves butterflies. "They buy the butterflies from a farm," she says, "and her husband mounts and frames them." You Google "Butterfly Farms" and discover one is an hour's drive away. Tours are available by appointment. There are presentations about Monarch butterflies and their life cycle, a "dress-up demonstration representing the anatomy of the butterfly." It is the perfect gift you can give to your granddaughter when she visits, as she does each summer, in August, when it likely will be safer to fly.

8

You research thyroid cancer and discover there are four kinds: Papillary, Follicular, Medullary, and Anaplastic. Papillary is the most common and has the best outlook because it grows slowly. Even when this cancer spreads to the lymph nodes, it responds well to treatment. Follicular and medullary are less common, but their prognosis is good overall. Anaplastic is the fastest-growing type of thyroid cancer, and it doesn't respond well to treatment.

9

Two months pass before your biopsy is rescheduled for the week after your Pennsylvania county and the one in which the hospital is located both go from "red" to "yellow."

10

Your neighbor, the prison guard, hosts a pandemic lockdown party. Five cars arrive. Each one has a prison parking sticker in the upper right-hand corner of its windshield. Though the weather is perfect for late May, clear and warm, all of the couples, neither the men nor the women wearing masks, go inside the house. You don't hear loud music; no one emerges onto the back patio. Because you have been inside that house, you know it is smaller than yours, that twelve adults and the guard's two children make a crowd.

11

You arrive for the cell extraction that will name the future. You tug your mask, that recent habit replacing fingers to the face or the temptation to examine, low along your throat, for invasion's tenderness or pain. When your glasses fog, you take them off and wave them clear while you slow your breathing. At the door to the hospital, you are asked for your name and birthday. Your temperature is taken while you submit to a brief inquest about recent contacts, shortness of breath, and persistent cough. The last question is whether or not three months of stay-at-home has, by now, seduced your restlessness.

Intimacy has been on such an extended leave, you nearly welcome the doctor's blue-sheathed hand, your throat softly touched and swept sideways for a needle so thin the myth of "only a pinch" comes true. You recognize extraction's pressure, the impulse to swallow throughout each attempt.

12

The butterfly farm also offers butterfly releases for special events, including weddings, anniversaries, birthdays, graduations, and memorials. Besides the ones from "mass release boxes," the farm promises special releases from individual envelopes that can be personalized with writing and a small picture.

The advertisement ends by saying that all metamorphic stages and butterfly releases are available, dependent upon season.

13

After each needle extraction, you wait to learn whether the sample has sufficient cells to be useful for a definitive assessment. Four samples are each, in turn, deemed insufficient. As if the pandemic has complicated biopsy, the aisles in your tumor designated one-way like the ones at your grocery store, the cells reluctant to emerge from lockdown because everyone is dangerous.

The doctor and the radiologist apologize while the technician carries your fifth sample to pathology. For now, the doctor says, it ends, because "we don't want to beat you up with more than five extractions." Before you leave, you learn that the chorus of your body's song has only repeated "non-diagnostic, but statistically safe." To be more certain, another biopsy should be scheduled. Though during these times, scheduling is difficult. Though weeks will likely pass.

Which is time enough for uncertainty to startle you from sleep like a dry, persistent cough. Which happens often enough for you to master the art of settling down. Slowly deep-breathing, you tell yourself, each time, that all three of those medical faces would be as unrecognizable as yours if you accidentally meet, unmasked in the open. Your throat will look so common they will never remember the mayhem of your small, ambiguous illness.

14

Your father never mentioned the process for pinning and preserving. The butterflies simply hung there like family portraits, the only ornamentation on the basement walls except for a framed print of a painting of the Titanic sinking that he hung on another wall after your grandmother died and none of your uncles or aunts wanted it.

15

The butterfly farm web site notes that you can purchase from any stage of the butterfly life cycle: eggs, larvae, pupae, or butterflies.

16

When there is another indoor party at your neighbor's house, this one attracting more cars, you write a brief story that you title "My Father, the Prison Guard":

> My father, the prison guard, says his cells have been opened now, the men he watches going home the same way he does. He says the Governor has freed them, not the virus. He has all the proof he needs—the prison is near the state capital and not one of the inmates is sick.
>
> My father's friends are guards, too. Three of them visited last week. They brought their wives, but not their children. My father said their names and ours. He said we're not afraid in this house. We're not distancing, not my wife, not my son and daughter. Masks are for thieves.
>
> The guests stayed for hours. My mother and the wives, after dinner, sat outside. They drank wine and looked at their phones. They texted their babysitters and told my mother, "Don't tell our husbands."
>
> The men drank beer and played poker. They bragged about how they've memorized the odds, how they can read each other's tells. I watched from behind my father. He took a sip of beer when his cards were good. He picked at the label when he bluffed.
>
> My brother and I stayed up past midnight. We watched a show where the host was at home and the audience was as far away as

we were. He made fun of men who refused to wear masks, but nobody was there to laugh.

When they were ready to leave, my father hugged his friends. Each one touched his face and laughed. My father repeated, "Trust is love." He sounded like our priest.

After the house was empty, my father said, "You kids see what strong is? Did you?" He hugged our mother and said, "Say thank you. Say it now before you see how right I am."

This week, every morning, my mother took my temperature. She took my brother's and hers, too, but only after my father left for work. "You keep this a secret," she said. "You tell me if you hear your father cough."

Today, while we ate breakfast, my father cleared his throat and said, "This thing will pass." He pulled the thermometer from his pocket and laid it on the table between our cereal boxes. He told us to take a good long look while he cleared his throat again.

"OK," he said. He picked it up and pointed it at our mother. "Your mother wants to take my temperature," he said. My mother bowed her head, but she didn't fold her hands or move her lips. He pointed the thermometer at my brother. "I told her to go ahead and try." He pointed it at me. "How's that sound?" he said. "Like I mean it?"

When my mother whimpered his name, he snapped the thermometer. "How's that sound?' he said, his voice hoarse. "Like the end of something?" None of us moved while he stood up. "I have work to do," he said. "That's what they're paying me for. Being there. Somebody they can count on."

17

Stage I-II thyroid cancers are confined to the thyroid. If it has spread to nearby lymph nodes, it is still considered stage I-II when the patient is younger than forty-five. The presence of cancer in the lymph nodes does not worsen the prognosis for younger patients.

Stage III thyroid cancer is greater than four cm in diameter and is limited to the thyroid or may have minimal spread outside the thyroid. Lymph nodes near the trachea may be affected. Stage III thyroid cancer that has spread to adjacent cervical tissue or nearby blood vessels has a worse prognosis. However, lymph node metastases do not worsen the prognosis for patients younger than forty-five.

Stage IV thyroid cancer has spread from your thyroid gland to other parts of your neck, lymph node or distant areas of your body like your lung or bones.

18

After you tell your wife you've missed the age advantage for thyroid cancer by thirty years. she says, "Your age matters more to the coronavirus."

19

To pin a butterfly, first gently press the thorax with the blunt end of a pair of tweezers until you feel and hear it crush. Be careful not to squash the thorax completely. Push a pin through the thorax so that where the wings join it is level with the top of the pinning board. Pin thin strips of card on either side of the body. Place a pin next to the abdomen on one side to keep the body in place while you open the wing. Using tweezers, move it into the position you desire. Press down gently. Be careful not to rip it as you hold the wing in position. Place a piece of unwaxed paper over the wing and pin around the outside. Repeat on the other side. Leave the specimen in a cool, dry place for a week. Keep ants and other pests away by using surface spray in the area near your specimen. Once it is dry, remove the pins and store it in a safe place. Use plenty of moth balls.

20

Your doctor's office is across the street from a nursing home that is shuttered, its parking lot secured from traffic with what appears to be crime scene tape. You park and call the office number to announce your arrival and wait, as instructed, by your car. After ten minutes, the midday sun brings up sweat and you call again. After fifteen minutes, you sit in your car, running the air conditioning and listening to music. You are startled when the receptionist raps on the window, and you step outside, unmasked, so close to her that she retreats. Over six months has passed since the original, postponed ultrasound appointment, more than three months since the ultrasound showed significant growth. The doctor orders a second biopsy. The appointment you have kept lasts less than ten minutes.

21

After five years, survival rates:

Papillary thyroid cancer: Regional - 99%, Distant - 78%

Follicular thyroid cancer: Regional - 96%, Distant - 63%

Medullary thyroid cancer: Regional - 90%, Distant - 39%

Anaplastic thyroid cancer: Regional - 12%, Distant - 4%

Just below that fourth, dismal prognosis, the site says: Remember, everyone is different. Ask your doctor what you can expect based on your type of cancer and other things that are unique to you.

You don't mention the numbers to your wife, keeping even the good numbers to yourself.

22

One morning, to distract yourself, you weed around the yard's shrubbery. Because you have forgotten to prune, for the second consecutive year, the butterfly bush your granddaughter loves towers far beyond repair, its leaves, during a dry July, gone uniformly curled and brown. Your granddaughter will not witness the result of your shoddy maintenance. The pandemic has canceled her late summer visit, furloughing you from discovery like a wealthy, white-collar felon.

23

The butterfly farm's site declares that although butterflies know when they are touched, it is thought that their nervous system does not have receptors that register pain "as we know it."

24

Your prison-guard story is accepted for publication. In 2021, the emailed contract says, which seems so distant, you simply type "ok, thanks" and click "send" after supplying a virtual signature.

25

A woman who appears to be as old as you are performs the second biopsy. She is cheerful in a grandmotherly way and describes out loud everything she is doing, "Now I am preparing to insert the needle. Soon you will feel pressure. There, now, the needle is doing its work...." She says she does five extractions in a row, sending all of them to the lab after she's finished because this biopsy is being performed in an auxiliary unit of the hospital. Even on the fifth extraction, she says, "Now I am preparing to insert the needle."

26

Your father, at eighty-eight, had his caregiver bring the Titanic print up from the basement and lay it on the dining room table. He asked you if you wanted it, saying it must be valuable because it was an antique by now. You didn't mention that years ago you'd seen that print on the walls of two friends' living rooms, the row boats surrounded by hopeless swimmers in the ocean, the *Titanic* listing steeply, poised to sink with passengers still on board. He never offered the butterflies, both of which were discarded after he died, no takers for either them or the Titanic, which, two years later, was still on the dining room table after he went to the nursing home.

27

In mid-August, over eight months since the original ultrasound appointment, you are told that the nodule that has grown is benign. The immediate concern is whether it will continue to grow and interfere with swallowing or speech. You are placed, once again, on a six-month ultrasound cycle.

28

In Los Angeles, your granddaughter begins school online. When you talk with her on FaceTime, you tell her about the butterfly farm and promise to take her next summer.

29

Walking home from the community pool on the Saturday before school in your town begins, the neighbor girl passes on the sidewalk. She smiles and waves. At once, you raise your hand to acknowledge her, so pleased you almost call out a question about the masks she will begin wearing to class, what sort of patterns she's chosen for sixth grade.

30

Late in your wife's latest Zoom book club meeting, during the goodbyes from isolation, you hear Denise say to everyone, "Would you like to see our butterfly collection?" You step into the room and watch as she tilts her laptop so the camera shows the dining room wall behind her is nearly covered with hung boxes of butterflies. You count twelve, nine in each box. 108 butterflies that look identical to you. You search the eight other women's faces in the Zoom panels, looking for a match to your wonder. Two go dark.

Denise stands, the room swaying through her camera as she carries the laptop closer to the wall. All of the butterflies seem to have the same deep blue with golden specks in a simple, consistent pattern. "They have names," she says, beginning a slow pan across the boxes. "They're on the back." Four panels are vacant.

"My husband is in self-quarantine," Denise says, "but so far, he's mild." She moves her laptop closer to the wall, holds it steady. You think of an atlas you once owned, how the biggest cities were enlarged in panels. You and your wife are alone with her as she says, "Don't they look as if they could fly?"

You imagine another wall sprouting something like an ivy of boxes before Denise hosts another Zoom book club meeting. What she will show and call beauty's still life while those others at the meeting go quickly dark into their ordinary, private lives. You vow to look up the species. To ask her now seems taboo, an interruption of worship. You imagine her husband busy with a new specimen, carefully restoring something dry and fragile under a brilliant light. While you stare and stare, all that is left of her is breathing.

Preservations

1

The Italian restaurant, on a weekday night, was nearly empty, and those few customers looked to be around my father's age, seventy-seven. If they were nostalgic, they'd likely share my father's romance with big band tunes, but the ceiling speakers crooned a piped-in selection of doo-wop songs. My father ate with gusto, but I liked the music better than the mediocre Italian food. I owned hundreds of doo-wop records. My father, nearly deaf, was oblivious, but he told me three times how miraculous his open-heart surgery had been, how those doctors could fix anything these days.

As I walked the bill to the register, the song that was playing was "High on a Hill" by Scott English. "I love this song," the waitress said as she rang me up.

"Me, too," I said, suddenly happy that someone else was paying attention to a song that had seldom been played anywhere else but on a few Pittsburgh radio stations. "It's fantastic."

My father had already wandered outside, but I lingered by the mints and toothpicks until the song ended. The waitress waited, too. When I finally stepped out beside him, my father asked, "There a problem with the check?"

"No, we're good."

He seemed distracted, suddenly anxious. "You like it, that place?"

"It's ok."

"Not fancy enough for you? I come here with your sister. She always says she likes it."

I let it go. I'd heard "High on a Hill" for the first time in years, and that made up for spaghetti with clam sauce dumped straight from a can. By the time I'd graduated from high school, doo-wop had become an oldies genre, a remnant that trailed behind my generation as it aged in the way Benny Goodman and Duke Ellington followed my father. Something to be preserved.

2

As various vegetables and fruits came into season, my mother preserved jars of them to store on shelves in the dank room she called the "root cellar." She labored over tomatoes and peaches, green beans and beets. Steam filled the kitchen, a side effect of sterilizing to make certain none of us would be victims of botulism. By summers end, the shelves were packed with preserves, jars that disappeared one by one until another cycle of canning began. After she died, my father ate what remained except for two unlabeled and undated jars that sat on the otherwise emptied shelves for nearly ten years. Whatever she had preserved sometimes looked like a fetus or a jumble of organs, but always something kept in formaldehyde.

3

Who isn't taken by stories like the one about M. Boulard, who owned seven houses, keeping a hundred thousand books in each of them? Or Richard Heber, who believed he needed three copies of every published volume, eight houses in three countries necessary to hold them. Reading those numbers, who doesn't decide there's likely no limit for hoarders of books, someone like Sir Thomas Phillips, whose goal was to own every book in the world.

4

My neighbor, once, bought books by the thousands, clearing out sales from garages and front yards to fill his basement floor to ceiling, starting, the year he invited me to admire what he kept, on rooms left vacant by his daughters grown and gone, arranging, by then, nearly a hundred thousand in chronological order to create, he said, the twentieth century of books.

Downstairs, I imagined fire beginning in the '40s or '50s; upstairs, collapse, his house imploded by a billion pages. I stood beside him in his younger daughter's bedroom, the '90s surrounding us. In the adjoining bedroom, the '80s had swollen the space nearly shut. My neighbor swept his large hands apart as if he were showing me stars, the infinite sprawled and demanding to be seen. A second, then two, he held them wide until I managed, "It's something," before I left, stepping back into the driveway where his station wagon sat low and stacked, a boxcar promising the raw materials of archiving.

5

When I retired, the archivist at the university where I taught created an organized space for me. My old neighbor, dead, by then, for more than a decade, would have approved. What I had published was being preserved, no longer heirlooms on shelves or in boxes inside my house. Every published word, even the mostly embarrassing poems that appeared in mimeographed, stapled magazines in the 1970s. The boxes in the room slid out like mausoleum "storage." I noticed ones labeled with the names of former presidents and trustees and professors. It felt like a specialized cemetery populated by strangers whose stories were already barely remembered.

6

Visiting the Mermaid Cemetery, I immediately noticed that someone regularly tended every grave. Someone carried kelp and seaweed to vases brimmed with water I tested with fingertips, learning the salt. The pages of the brochure were so damp, they curled. Already, the photographs of the interred were smeared. I followed the mulched trail among headstones shaped like fish, wishing myself a mourner, someone willing to accept a measure of loss in order to be transformed, scales swallowing my flesh until my body, fused into the elusive beauty of myth, eased into water, impossible enough for worship.

7

In a cathedral in Florence, surrounded by icons, I heard a loud, recorded "*Shhh*" swirl from above. A single "*Silencio*" followed. Through ear buds I listened to the near-whisper of the guide. Soon, "*Shhh,*" warned twice more, "*Silencio*" seemed the voice of a striking clock. Beside a roped-off sarcophagus, the guide murmured that a famous saint was so selfless her body was shared by cathedrals in competing cities. Here, the thumb survived, preserved as saints often are, by goodness. A woman from our group dipped her fingers into an ornate basin and moved her dripping hand through the sign of the cross. The guide paused to bow her head, suddenly obedient in the ancient, natural light.

8

My father's rotary telephone kept going for the entire fifty-seven years he lived in the house I grew up in. When, at ninety, he surrendered to senior care, I picked up the receiver and called my house, hearing the landline in the distant kitchen ringing. When voice mail asked me for a message, I could barely speak.

9

For ten years, each time I visited, my father spoke about how, though he was the oldest, he had outlasted his four siblings. What's more, they had died in reverse order of their age. Throughout his 80s, he seemed stunned to be the survivor. After the last of four funerals, I drove him up the steep, cobblestoned street to his old neighborhood where the houses huddled like the elderly had at the grave. He watched the windows of his house as if expecting his sister and three brothers to wave.

When I was a boy, viewings of the family's dead were held in the "parlor" of that house—an uncle, my grandmother, and finally, my grandfather, who was laid out three days in the deep gray suit he wore on Sundays. Knowing that the house would soon be sold, I explored before the funeral, nineteen and opening drawers and closets before the coffin would be struggled down the steep steps to Ogrodnik's sleek hearse. I climbed to the attic where, years before, it served as a barracks for those four brothers. I had seen a photo of them as teenage boys and young men arranged on cots as if already in basic training for the imminent war three of them would fight in. I tried to enter my father's life, kneeling to look through the one small window, trying to make out what he had witnessed in nineteen forty-one, in late November, his wedding a week away. I smeared a space and saw the abandoned steel mill at the base of the hill, the nearby hillside scarred when a bypass around the town had been constructed. I was sweating in my white shirt and blue tie, squinting while I wiped my brow with the back of my hand, unknowingly marking myself with dust, taking nothing downstairs to the viewing except a small sign of the stubborn past, wearing it with my one gray suit.

10

My father showed me his oldest dead brother's suits, six of them he had hung in the guest closet. Like a clerk, he displayed them one by one, lifting each to the light for approval. Four were dark—black, gray, brown, navy blue—the others, sewn from lighter cloth, were tan and a pastel green. I remembered seeing my uncle in that suit. He had worn it with white shoes as if he'd brought Florida to dinner. "You're about his size," my father said, "and he bought only quality," meaning he expected me to welcome them as an opportunity. When I hesitated, forming an excuse, he said, "Don't worry. They'll always be there. They'll keep."

11

A family, once, looked for skulls on their vacations and kept one of them to display in their home. If none were discovered, they substituted road kill that they buried in their yard until its coveted skull emerged. The family believed the skulls would carry the animal's spirit and personality to their shelves and walls—rabbit and skunk, possum, raccoon, squirrel, fox. The father, eventually, declared he wanted to leave his skeleton to his children. Stop joking, his wife said, fearing her children were so crazy for skulls that they might home-exhibit his boiled bones like a relic, the domestic taboo passed down like a singular, mutant gene.

12

For decades, the John Wilkes Booth Mummy traveled the country, attracting paying customers with its taboo thrill. It arrived near Pittsburgh, my great-uncle told me, when he was thirteen. In the tent's half-light, that body sported what was claimed to be the Ford's Theater suit. "A nickel's worth," my great-uncle said, a man who kept World War I to himself, preserving his uniform in a trunk except for dressing for his veteran's place in Pittsburgh's twice-a-year parades.

13

A woman fluttered among the visitors at the Angel Museum, glittery in her gold robe, keeping her white wings folded like a luminescent moth at rest. Some of the angels on display were constructed from stone. In all sizes, some were made of wood and gilt cardboard. Intricate ones shaped from paper were arranged on a series of full shelves. Just before closing, a bus idled in the parking lot. My wife and I were surrounded by the elderly, many, I was sure, younger than we were. They carried tiny angels they had created from ribbon and tissues and directions recited earlier by that angel. Eight canes rested in an umbrella stand just inside the door as a courtesy. Two of those tourists used a walker. One rode in a wheelchair. There was so much imminence, so close, that the near future almost collapses my knees. I felt shamed by my smile and flagrantly empty hands.

14

During the early weeks of the pandemic, my wife persuaded me to empty several sets of shelves of sports trophies I'd earned. There were a few softball and volleyball trophies, some old high school track medals, but the tennis trophies were the centerpiece of the what I placed on the carefully covered basement pool table. There were eighty-nine of them. I counted twice to be sure, hoping for ninety, disappointed somehow. Then, just after my wife came downstairs to photograph them—her promise had been part of the deal I'd made to further our downsizing—she noticed one more trophy that was lying on its side on the top shelf, discovering it only because she climbed two steps on our three-step ladder to dust. I had her photograph from three angles—it seemed important somehow—but after an hour on display like an embalmed well-dressed body, they went into garbage bags, all of them fatalities, no exceptions.

15

The morning after our meal in the Italian restaurant, the first televised news story was a fatal shooting in a notorious section of Pittsburgh. "Always the same," my father said, but the second story was about an explosion the night before that had destroyed that restaurant. The devastation had occurred around 9:30, four hours after we'd left and an hour and a half after it closed. My father was dumbfounded. "What are they talking about? We were just there."

I knew what he was thinking. The restaurant wasn't in the city, let alone in a part of town where violence was commonplace. It didn't have a bar that attracted the bad behavior he associated with those who "like their drink." Insurance fraud, I thought. Some sketchy financing gone wrong. "That doesn't make sense," he said. "It sits right there in a nice place. You can see all around it, lots of space."

I imagined the owner waiting for the restaurant to clear before he set things in motion. How he kept telling himself this extensive, financial surgery would fix his problems. Whether he listened to those overhead oldies while he worked. Whether he had labored in silence, intent upon getting the illusion of accident exactly right. Whether, before she'd left, he'd given that old-fashioned mix tape to the waitress who loved doo-wop so those songs would be stored in a safe place by someone who loved them.

Before I had to leave, I drove him, as always, to see the old places. On the way back, my father said, without prompting, "There's what's left of the house where I was born." I slowed and looked to my right, but there was nothing but vacant lots. He pointed, and I followed his finger to six concrete steps set into the hill that rose from the widened shoulder to the plateau of milkweed and sumac and wild berry tangled and brown from the summer before. "Right there where the steps go." The enormous machinery of road construction sat a hundred yards away. Before too long, most likely within days, those steps would be gone as well, but right now they nearly shimmered with presence. "Like nothing was ever there," my father said. By then we were turning, as always, at the Eat 'n Park. Neither of us spoke while we drove up the hill to his house.

16

On the street just above ours, a house was rebuilt exactly the same as it was before a total-loss fire. The owner explained that she had cloned her house from photographs and blueprints that survived in a fireproof, padlocked box. After the house was filled with furniture, the owner's mother, in her 90s, sat in the same model of chair in the identical spot in the living room to watch television whose volume was set at the same level of loudness as before the fire, one that allowed her to hear.

17

Sometimes the slender grace of extraordinary can be heard where tragedy seems inevitable. At extremely north latitudes, in winter, there are consequences from exposing even the smallest parts of the body to a moment of weather, but on the coldest of days, the breath expelled with a spoken sentence can be briefly suspended in ice, hovering until the whisper of stars is overheard, what Siberians call the tinkling crash of those frozen words, their delicate beauty provided by rare, yet bearable cold.

18

The story, each time the biologist told it, elicited laughter. Because January's below-zero days meant the English professor who named her pets after women writers could not open ground to bury Jane Austen, her latest dead cat, beside years of others in her backyard, she brought the boxed cat to his office. Caught off-guard, he'd agreed to store it inside his department's freezer, donating a few months of preservation, but by April he had forgotten it and so had she, her elderly parents, who lived with her, both failing, her house a distraction of rescued dogs. *Well,* he would say, dramatically pausing, *seven years passed.* A new science building meant a move of specimens from freezer to freezer, and there was the cat, somewhat worse for wear, that woman, by then, about to retire, and he had flung it, still boxed, into the dumpster provided for transition's casualties.

The last time I heard him tell that story, everyone listening knew that woman had lost her place in the world, her mind relocated near childish dependency. By then, though no one interrupted, a few of us wondered why he couldn't have driven that coffin home, using some remote part of his own back yard for burial.

19

For years, perfectly preserved, Lenin's unburied body has been a public icon in Russia. During World War II, it was moved from St. Petersburg and hidden in Tyumen. Germans were nearing St. Petersburg, but in Siberia, anything could be hidden—artwork, political prisoners, a tomb so successfully kept a secret for so long that there were nights when the guards, lonely for usefulness, drank themselves into sorrowful songs. While Lenin waited for worshippers, those men woke to a noon of half-light upon the long-winter landscape, pale and shallow like fog that will not break for days, as persistent as siege.

20

At Rocky Flats, where plutonium detonators were made, one chamber became so contaminated it was called The Infinity Room for how long the siege of its poison would last.

21

Twenty years ago, I learned that Silly Putty will last and last. "It's indestructible," an expert proclaimed, estimating that ten million pounds of that gunk lay in landfills, lakes, and the basements of abandoned houses. "Because the putty mimics the specific gravity of our flesh," he said, "we empathize with the probable permanence of that toy."

22

Vitrification is the term for how nearly permanent nuclear waste is melted with glass beads in furnaces and poured into steel boxes to become blocks of radioactive glass that need to be very carefully buried. Absolute necessity? Twenty feet wide, a space once opened in the roof of a Hanford tunnel where nuclear waste is stored, robots sent to test and repair, eight feet of soil prescribed to prevent an airborne radiological event escaping a tunnel that holds railroad cars of radioactive waste, literally, that summer, seventy-five years young, my mother's phrase for the old, yet active, an age she did not reach to verify its truth

23

My mother's father, for the last twenty-five years of his life, created throw rugs from what seemed to be perfectly selected, colorful rags. Acquaintances at the charity home where he spent those years gave him old shirts and pants and even suits to cut up and weave. Everyone said he had a knack for how they went together, stitching up those remnants so nobody could even tell where one scrap started and another ended. "That's about all that's left of your grandfather," my father would say, "that and all the stories about what the drink does to a man."

A lifelong binge drinker, he'd lost jobs, wrecked a car, punched holes in the wall of his house, but what had made my grandmother throw him out for good was stealing the three silver dollars my mother had won in a local eighth-grade essay-writing contest.

"The drink makes a fool out of people," my father often repeated. "He only made these rugs after he ended up in the charity home with nothing but the shirt on his back." The rug in my sister's old room lay in place for half a century, a multi-colored whirlpool, including a swirl of patterns that must have originally been a woman's dress or maybe some man's Hawaiian shirt. Some small bit of what was no longer useful made valuable.

24

Ten years after my father offered the use of my uncle's suits, they were hung inside plastic bags when he showed them to me again. "Your boys are grown now," he said. "Maybe they want them."

"I'll ask," I said, using ambivalence for a placeholder.

"Do that," he said. "You can see I've made sure they're safe."

25

In his overstuffed garage, my father kept a safe where he stored mementoes that he believed were so valuable they needed extra security. Once a year, he moved it— left, then right, then back again behind lawnmowers, screens, and four sets of hoses in the open vault of the crowded garage. The safe held Indian head pennies, buffalo nickels, and heavy silver dollars from the 19th century. There was a box of my mother's old jewelry. Locks from my first haircut, bits of initial nail clippings, and a set of lost baby teeth, enough of my early childhood for retrospective voodoo, were sealed in plastic.

26

Sealed in a crypt of urns, I've learned, are the hearts of twenty-two long-dead Popes. The latest Popes are buried whole, their hearts admitting "eventually" and "inevitably" and the rest of the adverbs of impermanence, while in Rome, those twenty-two hearts, well-guarded, sing the patient song of stone.

27

"This takes patience," my father said, "but it's worth it." We were in my sister's old room, another of my visits nearly over. On a card table was a large wooden board with slots that held, by my quick multiplication of row and columns, eighty-one slides. "I've been looking through all these," he said, pointing to the rest of the table's surface where a pile of slides, no way to exactly count them, was sprawled wide enough to suggest five-hundred or more. "Here," he said, "take a look. That's you in this one when you were a Boy Scout." Even held up to the light by the window, it was hard to make out what was in the tiny picture that seemed to cry out for magnification. "I used to watch these but the projector quit on me."

"We had an old hand-viewer way back."

"It's nowhere. I looked and so did your sister."

"It has to be here somewhere," I said, but my father didn't seem to hear. "It's in the house, Dad. Nobody ever throws anything away here."

"Your mother would know." Which seemed to settle things. Because she was dead, finding the viewer was impossible, its location a secret she'd taken to the grave.

In the cellar, twenty minutes later, I found the viewer in a box labeled "Toys." The light came on when I pressed the button. Upstairs again, I inserted a slide and handed the viewer to my father. "Push and look, Dad."

"There you are in your uniform just like I said." He laid the Scout slide back in place and inserted another, looking closely and at length before he handed it to me. "There we all are," he said. It was a photo of my father and his three brothers taken, by the looks of the car parked nearby, in the early 1960s. He took it back and looked again. I waited to give him time, but he replaced the slide and laid the viewer on the table.

The sun came out as we traveled the familiar roads before I had to leave. It was warm enough to imagine that Christmas wasn't five days away. Neither of us spoke until my father pointed at the windshield and said, "It's all gone up ahead."

"What?" I said, asking for clues.

"The mess they left behind at that Italian restaurant. It didn't take long once they got around to it."

My father stared straight ahead until we approached the site. There was nothing but patches of snow and mud. "See how it is?" my father said, sounding triumphant. "Like nothing was worth saving. Like it was never there."

28

My mother saved the photos left behind by dead relatives in six hat-box sized cans that originally held syrup-soaked peaches, cherries, or apples for my father's bakery pies. She accumulated thousands of formal poses or candid snapshots, the oldest become strangers, unidentified by aunts and uncles who knew those faces so well they never thought to caption them. For twenty-one years after she died, my father kept those cans buried in his basement like time capsules. When I opened them a few weeks before his move, at ninety, to a nursing home, he shook his head to the identity of every face, even my mother's as a child.

29

As children, everyone, until recently, learned cursive writing. My mother, the secretary, could write perfectly in longhand and shorthand, loops and slants exactly the same from message to message. For decades, she kept the books for my father's bakery, entering purchases in cursive so clear I could, years after her death and busy with investigating the past, identify every product like an auditor. Now, there are action groups for preserving cursive. Attending a meeting, I've watched a teacher write beautifully upon a blackboard. "Your handwriting reveals you to the world," she said, and though I believe what reveals is the exact arrangement of the words you choose, I was astonished by the symmetry of her sample lines, her ease with what passes, by now, for calligraphy.

30

For twenty-one years, in calligraphy my sister paid for, my poem grounded in the recollection of my mother's death hung framed and under glass in my father's living room. Each time I visited, before he closed his eyes and faced away, he asked me to proofread while he recited the poem's thirty-one lines, preserving what he considered perfection.

31

Our cremains will weigh from six to ten pounds, the preserved fragments white or gray, the largest pieces ground to sand-size for discretion and the ease of scattering. Not comforting, this summary, but better, pre-need, than anticipating decomposition by traditional burial. Better yet, post-burning options have been created to lessen despair for the living—etched keepsake urns, ash-speckled cards, jewelry that carries cremains near the wrists, the throat or the heart.

Moreover, scattering the ashes is more romantic than burial. A multitude of sites have appeal—at sea, in a meadow, a favorite grove in a forest. Or, because height is often craved—off a cliff or the balcony of the dead's high-rise apartment. From airplanes, from helicopters and hot-air balloons, even expelled from the raised barrel of a shotgun to ensure a high arc of dust. And lately, with fireworks, those ashes blown into rainbows to ooohs and aaahs from the living.

Now, the launch into space, a years-long orbit until small meteors of ash plummet again into burning. And those who will pay for lift-off to the moon and Mars, or the infinite ride beyond solar system borders, escaping even the great scenario of ash, how the Earth, in a billion years, will become a planet of dust. How, finally, it will spiral into the huge, expanding sun, which, while dying, will scatter Earth, rendering all of our cremains to swirling in eternal memorial, perfecting grief, at last, because there's never enough preserving, never enough remembering as we fling those we love in wide, then wider arcs, as if distance can resurrect the dead, create an image we're able to see when we're alone, concentrating on some speck of sky as we breathe the heavenly dust of the loved.

Acknowledgements

The essays in this collection appeared, sometimes in a somewhat different form, in the following journals:

Kenyon Review Online, Quarterly West, American Literary Review, Brevity, Pleiades, Shenandoah, The Gettysburg Review, On the Seawall, december, Lake Effect, Bio Stories, Woven Tale Review, South Dakota Review, Connotation Press, Bending Genres, World Literature Today, Citron Review, and *Sweet Lit.*

"After the Three-Moon Era" was reprinted in *Best American Essays 2020.*

"Telephone" was cited as a Notable Essay by *Best American Essays 2022.*

"Faith" received a Pushcart Prize Citation for Nonfiction.

"Consolations" and "The History of Hair" were reprinted in *The Cresset.*

About the Author

Gary Fincke is the winner of the 2003 Flannery O'Connor Award for Short Fiction, the 2003 Ohio State University/The Journal Poetry Prize, the 2005 Arkansas Poetry Prize, the 2010 Stephen F. Austin Poetry prize, the 2015 Jacar Press Poetry Prize, the 2015 Elixir Press Fiction Prize, the 2017 Robert C. Jones Prize for Nonfiction, and the 2018 Wheelbarrow Books (Michigan State) Poetry Prize. Since 1984, he has published forty books of poetry, short fiction, and nonfiction, including collections of essays from Michigan State and Stephen F. Austin as well as the memoir *Amp'd: A Father's Backstage Pass,* an account of immersing himself in his younger son's life as the lead guitarist of the platinum-selling rock band Breaking Benjamin.

His work has appeared in such periodicals as *Harper's, The Paris Review, The Kenyon Review, The Georgia Review, American Scholar, The Gettysburg Review, The Missouri Review, Black Warrior Review, Ploughshares, Arts & Letters,* and *DoubleTake.* Twice awarded Pushcart Prizes, he has been recognized by *Best American Stories* and the O. Henry Prize series, and cited eighteen times in the past twenty-one years for a "Notable Essay" in *Best American Essays.*

"After the Three-Moon Era," the lead essay in The Mayan Syndrome, first published at *Kenyon Review Online,* was reprinted in *Best American Essays 2020.* His essay "The Canals of Mars," first published in Shenandoah, was reprinted in *The Pushcart Prize, XXV,* and subsequently reprinted again in *The Pushcart Essays,* an anthology of the best nonfiction from the first twenty-five years of the Pushcart Prize volumes.

Gary Fincke is the Emeritus Charles Degenstein Professor of Creative Writing at Susquehanna University, where he founded and then directed the Writers Institute and the nationally recognized undergraduate creative writing major, for more than two decades.

Made in the USA
Middletown, DE
25 October 2023

41306805R00149